BONHOEFFER

PASTOR, MARTYR, PROPHET, SPY

STUDENT EDITION

ERIC METAXAS

THOMAS NELSON
Since 1798

NASHVILLE   MEXICO CITY   RIO DE JANEIRO

Bonhoeffer Student Edition

© 2015 by Eric Metaxas

All rights reserved. No portion of this book may be reproduced, stored in a retrieval system, or transmitted in any form or by any means—electronic, mechanical, photocopy, recording, scanning, or other—except for brief quotations in critical reviews or articles, without the prior written permission of the publisher.

Published in Nashville, Tennessee, by Tommy Nelson. Tommy Nelson is an imprint of Thomas Nelson. Thomas Nelson is a registered trademark of HarperCollins Christian Publishing, Inc.

Adapted from *Bonhoeffer: Pastor, Martyr, Prophet, Spy*. Copyright © 2010 by Eric Metaxas. Also adapted from the abridged *Bonhoeffer: Pastor, Martyr, Prophet, Spy*. Copyright © 2014 by Eric Metaxas.

Photos used with permission from Art Resource, Eric Metaxas, Getty Images, and Shutterstock.

Scripture quotations marked NCV are taken from The Holy Bible, New Century Version®. Copyright © 2005 by Thomas Nelson, Inc. Scripture quotations marked NLT are taken from the Holy Bible. New Living Translation copyright © 1996, 2004, 2007, 2013 by Tyndale House Foundation. Used by permission of Tyndale House Publishers Inc., Carol Stream, Illinois 60188. All rights reserved. Scripture quotations marked NKJV are taken from The Holy Bible, New King James Version Copyright © 1982 by Thomas Nelson, Inc. Scripture quotations marked NIV are taken from the Holy Bible, New International Version®, NIV® Copyright © 1973, 1978, 1984, 2011 by Biblica, Inc.® Used by permission. All rights reserved worldwide. Scripture quotations marked RSV are taken from Revised Standard Version of the Bible, copyright © 1946, 1952, and 1971 the Division of Christian Education of the National Council of the Churches of Christ in the United States of America. Used by permission. All rights reserved.

Library of Congress Cataloging-in-Publication Data

Metaxas, Eric.
  Bonhoeffer : pastor, martyr, prophet, spy / Eric Metaxas. — Student Edition.
    pages cm
  Includes bibliographical references.
  ISBN 978-0-7180-2164-1 (softcover)
  1. Bonhoeffer, Dietrich, 1906–1945. 2. Theologians—Germany—Biography. 3. Clergy—Germany—Biography. 4. Righteous Gentiles in the Holocaust—Germany—Biography. 5. Spies—Germany—Biography. 6. Christian martyrs—Germany—Biography. 7. Bonhoeffer, Dietrich, 1906–1945—Political and social views. 8. Anti-Nazi movement—Germany. 9. Hitler, Adolf, 1889–1945—Assassination attempt, 1944 (July 20) 10. Germany—History—1933–1945—Biography. I. Title.
  BX4827.B57M48 2015
  230'.044092—dc23
  [B]   2014047618

Printed in the United States of America

15 16 17 18 19 20 RRD 6 5 4 3 2 1

Mfr. RRD / Crawfordsville / May 2015 / PO# 9342854

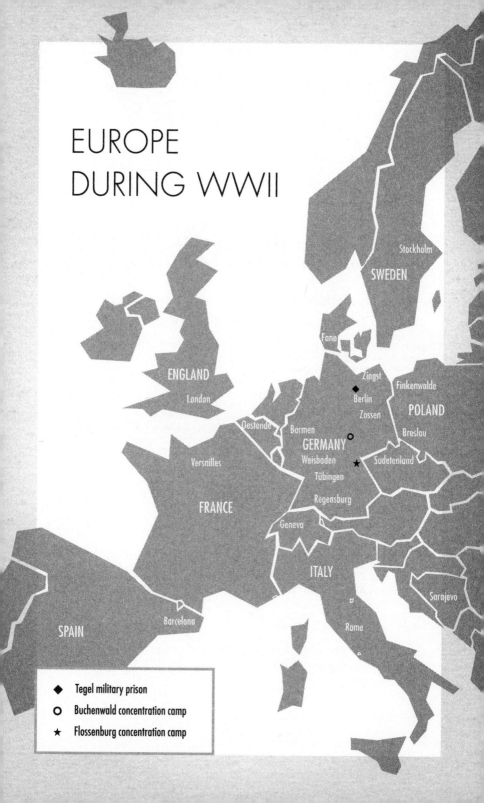

EUROPE
DURING WWII

Stockholm

SWEDEN

Fanø

ENGLAND

London

Zingst

Berlin

Finkenwalde

Zossen

POLAND

Oostende

Barmen

GERMANY

Breslau

Versailles

Weisbaden

Tübingen

Sudetenland

FRANCE

Regensburg

Geneva

ITALY

Sarajevo

Barcelona

Rome

SPAIN

◆ Tegel military prison

○ Buchenwald concentration camp

★ Flossenburg concentration camp

THE BONHOEFFER FAMILY TREE

Karl-Friedrich Bonhoeffer (1899–1957)
Margarete von Dohnanyi Bonhoeffer (1903–1992)

Karl Walter (1931)

Friedrich (1932)

Martin (1935)

Katharina (1937)

Walter Bonhoeffer
(1899–1918)

Klaus Bonhoeffer (1901–1945)
Emilie Delbruck Bonhoeffer (1905–1991)

Thomas (1931)

Cornelie (1934)

Walter (1938)

Ursula Bonhoeffer Schleicher (1902–1983)
Rudiger Schleicher (1895–1945)

Hans-Walter (1924)

Renate Schleicher Bethge (1925)
Eberhard Bethge

Dorothee (1928)

Christine (1903)

Karl Bonhoeffer (1868–1948)
Paula von Hase Bonhoeffer (1874–1951)

Dietrich Bonhoeffer (1906–1945)
(engaged to Maria von Wedemeyer)

Christine Bonhoeffer von Dohnanyi (1903–1965)
Hans von Dohnanyi (1902–1945)

Barbara (1926)

Christoph (1929)

Klaus (1928)

Sabine Bonhoeffer Leibholz (1906–1999)
Gerhard Leibholz (1901–1982)

Marianne (1927)

Christiane (1930)

Susanne Bonhoeffer Dress (1909–1991)
Walter Dress (1904–1979)

Michael (1935)

Andreas (1938)

CONTENTS

Chapter 1: The End, 1945   1

Chapter 2: A Mischievous Boy and the Great War, 1896–1921   7

Chapter 3: Off to University, 1923–1927   23

Chapter 4: Venturing Abroad, 1928–1930   33

Chapter 5: A New Way of Seeing the Church, 1930–1933   43

Chapter 6: Nazi Lies, 1933   53

Chapter 7: Worshiping God . . . or Hitler?, 1933–1934   73

Chapter 8: Secret Seminaries, 1934–1937   93

Chapter 9: Rumblings of War, 1937–1939   115

Chapter 10: The Great Decision, 1939   131

Chapter 11: From Pastor to Spy, 1940–1942   141

Chapter 12: Meeting Maria, 1942–1943   157

Chapter 13: Cell 92, 1943–1944   167

Chapter 14: The Conspiracy Fails, 1944–1945   185

Chapter 15: On the Road to Freedom, 1945   197

Chapter 16: The Martyr, 1945   215

List of Key Words and People   221

Notes   231

About the Author   245

CHAPTER 1

THE END

JULY 27, 1945, LONDON

We have troubles all around us, but we are not defeated. We do not know what to do, but we do not give up the hope of living. We are persecuted, but God does not leave us. We are hurt sometimes, but we are not destroyed. We carry the death of Jesus in our own bodies so that the life of Jesus can also be seen in our bodies.

—2 CORINTHIANS 4:8–10 NCV

Peace had at last returned to Europe. The war that came to be known as World War II had been over for two months. The tyrant **Adolf Hitler*** took his own life in a gray bunker beneath his shattered capitol in Berlin, and the **Allies** declared victory.

Slowly, slowly, life in Britain turned to the task of rebuilding itself from the rubble. It was the first summer of peace in six years. But as if to prove that the whole thing hadn't been just a terrible nightmare, awful news kept pouring in. Evidence began to emerge of the **death camps** and the many other unspeakable acts carried out by the **Nazis** against millions of Jews—and anyone else who dared to go against them.

---

* Words in bold are defined in the List of Key Words and People at the back of the book.

The Axis vs. The Allies

World War II was fought between two sides known as the **Axis** and the Allies.

THE ALLIES

- Great Britain
- France (except during its German occupation from 1940–1944)
- United States
- Soviet Union
- China
- United Nations (including Australia, Belgium, Canada, China, Costa Rica, Cuba, Czechoslovakia, Dominican Republic, Greece, Guatemala, Haiti, Honduras, India, Luxembourg, the Netherlands, New Zealand, Nicaragua, Norway, Panama, Poland, Salvador, South Africa, Yugoslavia, the Philippines, Mexico, Ethiopia, Iraq, Free French, and Free Danes)

VS. THE AXIS

- Germany (also known as the Nazis, or the Third Reich)
- Italy
- Japan[1]

Rumors of such horrors had been whispered about throughout the war, but now they were confirmed by shocking photographs, newsreel footage, and eyewitness accounts from the soldiers who had freed the camps' prisoners during the last days of the war. The truth of all that the Nazis had done was worse than anyone had imagined. The world was stunned by the very evilness of the Nazis' evil.

At the beginning of the war, it had been possible to separate the Nazi government from the German people and to see that not all Germans were Nazis. But as the war raged

newsreel

(nuz‚rēl) : a short film that reported the news and that was shown in movie theaters in the past.[2]

on—and as more and more British fathers and sons and brothers died—telling the difference between Nazis and Germans became more difficult. British Prime Minister **Winston Churchill** decided to use this to his advantage during the fighting. By making the Germans and the Nazis into a single, hated enemy, he believed it would be easier to defeat them and put an end to the nightmare of the war.

But not all Germans were Nazis. Some Germans, known as the **German resistance**, were actually working inside Germany to defeat Hitler and the Nazis. The resistance reached out to Churchill and the British government for help. They hoped to work together with the British to defeat the Nazis, but they were turned away. The resistance wanted to tell the world that some Germans trapped inside Nazi Germany felt as much pain as the rest of the world did. But no one was interested in what they had to say. It was simply too late. Churchill thought it was simpler to tell the British people that there were no good Germans. Some even said that the only good German was a dead German.

But now the war was over. And even as the full evil of the Nazis' **Third Reich** was coming to light, the other side of things had to be seen too. Perhaps all Germans weren't evil after all.

And so on this day, July 27, 1945, in the Holy Trinity Church in London, a service was taking place that some people struggled to understand. For many it was deeply disturbing, especially for those who had lost loved ones during the war. This was because the memorial service being held this day on British soil was for a German who had died three months earlier. The news of his death had been hidden in the fog of war and was only now slowly becoming known. Most of his friends and family still knew nothing about it. But here in London there were gathered those few who did.

In the pews of the church sat the man's thirty-nine-year-old twin sister, her half-Jewish husband, and their two girls. It had been this man who had helped them slip out of Germany before the war, driving at night across the border into Switzerland. The dead man counted among his friends a number of important people, including **George Bell**, a bishop in the Church of England. It was Bell who had arranged the service, for he had known and loved the man being honored. They had met years before when they both worked to warn Europe about the Nazis' evil plans. Later, they had also worked together to try to rescue Jews and to bring the German resistance to the attention of the British government.

Far away in Berlin, the capital of Germany, in a three-story house, an elderly couple sat by their radio. Together, the couple had raised eight children, four boys and four girls. Their second son had been killed in the First World War. For a whole year, his young mother had been crushed by grief. Twenty-seven years later, a second war would take two more boys from her. Her husband was the most respected psychiatrist in Germany. And even though they knew it was dangerous, they had both spoken out against Hitler from the beginning. They were proud of their sons and sons-in-law who had worked to bring his evil reign to an end. But when the war ended at last, they didn't know what had happened to their sons. A month before they sat down by their radio, they had finally heard that their third son, **Klaus**, had been killed. But they still knew nothing about their youngest son, **Dietrich**. Then a neighbor told them that the **BBC radio** would broadcast a memorial service the next day from London. It was for Dietrich.

When the time for the service came, the old couple turned on their radio. As they listened, they took in the hard news that the good man who was their son was now dead. At the same time, many British people took in the hard news that the dead man—who was a German—was also a good man.

The man who died was engaged to be married. He was a pastor and a theologian. And he was executed for his role in the plot to **assassinate**—to kill—Adolf Hitler. The man's name was Dietrich Bonhoeffer. This is his story.

pastor (pas-tər) : a minister or priest in charge of a church or parish. In this case, also a *theologian*, or someone who is an expert on the study of God, faith, practice, and experience.

martyr (mär-tər) : a person who is killed or who suffers greatly for a religion or cause.

prophet (prä-fət) : a person who fortells or predicts what is to come; a spokesperson of some doctrine, cause, or movement.

spy (spī) : a person who tries secretly to get information about a country or organization for another country or organization.[3]

CHAPTER 2

A MISCHIEVOUS BOY AND THE GREAT WAR

1896–1921

The rich world of his ancestors set the standards for Dietrich Bonhoeffer's own life. It gave him a certainty of judgment and manner that cannot be acquired in a single generation.

—EBERHARD BETHGE

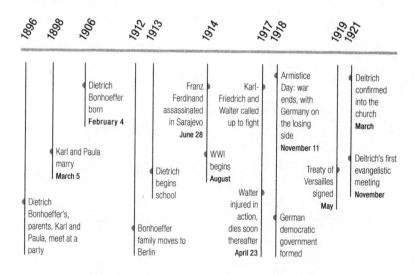

1896 · 1898 · 1906 · 1912 1913 · 1914 · 1917 1918 · 1919 1921

Dietrich Bonhoeffer born
February 4

Karl and Paula marry
March 5

Dietrich Bonhoeffer's, parents, Karl and Paula, meet at a party

Franz Ferdinand assassinated in Sarajevo
June 28

Dietrich begins school

Bonhoeffer family moves to Berlin

Karl-Friedrich and Walter called up to fight

WWI begins
August

Walter injured in action, dies soon thereafter
April 23

Armistice Day: war ends, with Germany on the losing side
November 11

Treaty of Versailles signed
May

German democratic government formed

Deitrich confirmed into the church
March

Deitrich's first evangelistic meeting
November

That old couple listening to the radio in 1945 met for the first time at a party in the winter of 1896. Their names were **Karl Bonhoeffer** and **Paula von Hase**. Years later, Karl wrote, "There I met a young, fair, blue-eyed girl . . . as soon as she entered the room she took me captive. This moment when I first laid eyes upon my future wife remains in my memory with an almost mystical force."[1]

Karl and Paula married on March 5, 1898, just three weeks before the groom's thirtieth birthday. The bride was twenty-two. He was a doctor, and she was a teacher. They both came from respected and well-known families.

Karl and Paula had eight children within ten years. Both **Karl-Friedrich** and **Walter** were born in 1899—one in January and the other in December. Their third son, Klaus, was born in 1901, followed by two daughters, **Ursula** in 1902 and **Christine** in 1903. On February 4, 1906, their fourth and youngest son, Dietrich, was born ten minutes before his twin sister, **Sabine**. He teased her about this head start throughout their lives. **Susanne**, the last child, was born in 1909. Dietrich was the only child to inherit his mother's fair skin and straw-colored hair. The others were dark like their father.

THE BONHOEFFER FAMILY

Karl Bonhoeffer (father) Paula von Hase Bonhoeffer (mother)	
Karl-Friedrich (1899)	Christine (1903)
Walter (1899)	Dietrich (1906)
Klaus (1901)	Sabine (1906)
Ursula (1902)	Susanne (1909)

Art Resource

This picture of the Bonhoeffer children and their governess was taken in about 1910. Karl and Paula Bonhoeffer stand in the background. Dietrich is just to the right of the governess.

All the Bonhoeffer children were born in the city of Breslau, Germany, which is now a part of Poland. There, Karl Bonhoeffer was head of **psychiatry** and **neurology** at the university, as well as director of a hospital for nervous diseases. The Bonhoeffers lived in a gigantic, rambling, three-story mansion with gabled roofs, lots of chimneys, a screened porch, and a balcony that overlooked a large garden where the children played.

The parents took great joy in their children and encouraged their interests. One room became a zoo for the children's pets, which included rabbits, guinea pigs, turtledoves, squirrels, lizards, and snakes. There were also collections of birds' eggs, mounted beetles, and butterflies. Another room was set up as a dolls' house for the girls. Still another room was the boys' workshop, complete with tools and a carpenter's bench.

Their mother was in charge of the home. Trusted governesses

helped look after the children, but it was Paula who taught them their lessons in an upstairs schoolroom. As a single woman, Paula had taken the teacher's examination. As a married woman, she used her skills to teach her young children. When they were a bit older, she sent them to the local public schools, where they made excellent grades.

Paula also oversaw the children's religious schooling. She felt it was important to teach them the basics of **theology**, which is the study of God and God's relation to the world in everyday life. Long before they knew that little Dietrich would grow up to be a pastor and theologian himself, they wrote down some of his earliest thoughts about God. Once, when he was about four years old, he asked his mother: "Does the good God love the chimney sweep too?" and "Does God, too, sit down to lunch?"[2]

What were your earliest thoughts about God? Do you have a memory of a prayer, a lesson, or a question you asked when you were young? Write it down here. One day your children might want to know!

_____

_____

_____

_____

_____

Though they believed in God, the Bonhoeffers rarely went to church. The family was not *against* the church—in fact, the children loved to "play" at baptizing each other—but their Christianity was mostly carried out at home. Daily life was filled with Bible reading and hymn singing, all of it led by Paula Bonhoeffer.

Paula Bonhoeffer's faith was clearly seen in the values that she and her husband taught their children. Selflessness, generosity, and helping others were very important in their family. Still, the children were not perfect. Their governess remembered this:

> Dietrich was often mischievous and got up to various pranks, not always at the [proper] time. I remember that Dietrich specially liked to do this when the children were supposed to get washed and dressed quickly because we had been invited to go out. So one such day he was dancing round the room, singing and being a thorough [pest]. Suddenly the door opened, his mother descended upon him, boxed his ears right and left, and was gone. Then the nonsense was over. Without shedding a tear, he now did what he ought.[3]

Though Karl Bonhoeffer would not have called himself a Christian, he respected his wife's desire to share her Christian beliefs with their children. Paula had grown up in a family that was devoted to God, and she was quite serious about her faith. Through her teachings and her example, she passed this faith down to all her children, especially Dietrich.

FAMILY VALUES

The Bonhoeffers' family values included: selflessness, generosity, helping others, and respecting others' thoughts and ideas. Are these important values in your family?

Over the coming years, the Bonhoeffers would face violence, hunger, and war. How might their faith in God and their family values have helped them to find moments of happiness in the middle of all their struggles?

THE MOVE TO BERLIN, 1912

In 1912, Dietrich's father took a job as the head of psychiatry and neurology in Berlin, at one of the world's best universities. This put him at the top of his field in all of Germany. The move to Berlin was a big change for the family. Their new house was

Eric Metaxas photo

The Bonhoeffer family moved to this house in Berlin in 1916. Today the vast house is divided into eight apartments.

not as grand as their old house, and their yard was smaller. But it had the honor of sharing a wall with Bellevue Park, where the royal princes and princesses played.

In 1913, seven-year-old Dietrich began school outside the home. He did well in school, but he was not beyond needing discipline, which his parents were quick to give. "Dietrich does his work naturally and tidily," his father wrote. "He likes fighting, and does a great deal of it."[4]

"HURRAH! THERE'S A WAR!"

After the move to Berlin, the Bonhoeffers spent the summer of 1914 in a country house in the mountains nearby. But on the first day of August, while the three younger children and their governess were in the village enjoying themselves, the world changed: Germany had declared war on Russia. For some time, tensions between the countries of the European continent had begun to rise as they each strived to gain more power and more land. Germany and Austria-Hungary had allied themselves against Russia and Serbia. So, when Austro-Hungarian Archduke **Franz Ferdinand** was assassinated in Serbia, those tensions exploded into a war that would quickly consume much of the world.

It was the beginning of the Great War, which would later come to be known as World War I. Dietrich and Sabine were eight and a half years old. Sabine remembered the scene:

> The village was celebrating its local shooting festival. Our governess suddenly dragged us away from the pretty, enticing market stalls and the merry-go-round which was being pulled by a poor white horse, so as to bring us back as quickly as possible to our parents in Berlin. . . . In the late evening we could hear through the window the songs and shouts of the soldiers in their farewell celebrations. Next day, after the adults had hastily done the packing, we found ourselves sitting in the train to Berlin.[5]

When the children arrived back home, one of the girls ran into the house and exclaimed, "Hurrah! There's a war!" She was firmly corrected. The Bonhoeffers were not completely against the war, but they would not celebrate it.

For the most part, however, the boys were thrilled, though they were more careful about showing it. Dietrich's brothers wouldn't turn eighteen and be able to fight in the army until 1917, which was three years away. No one dreamed the war could last that long. But they could at least get caught up in the whole thing and talk about it as the grown-ups did. Dietrich often played at soldiers with his cousins, and he collected newspaper articles about events at the front lines of the war. Like many boys, he made a map and stuck colored pins into it, marking the Germans' movements across Europe.

THE WAR COMES HOME

In time, though, the hard realities of war came home. A cousin was killed. Then another. Another cousin lost a leg. Another had an eye shot out and a leg severely crushed. Yet another cousin died. Food grew scarce. Even for the well-to-do Bonhoeffers, hunger became an issue. Dietrich turned out to be especially good at tracking down food supplies. In fact, his father praised him for his skill as a "messenger and food scout."[6] Dietrich even saved up his own money to buy a hen for eggs.

As the war continued, the Bonhoeffers heard of more deaths and injuries among their circle of friends. In 1917, their two oldest boys, Karl-Friedrich and Walter, were called to fight in the war. Walter had been preparing for this moment since the war broke out, taking long hikes with extra weights in his backpack to make himself stronger. Karl-Friedrich actually took his physics textbook to war with him. In 1917, things were still looking very well for Germany. They were confident they would win the war. Walter left home in April 1918. As the train was pulling away from the station, Paula Bonhoeffer ran alongside it, telling her son: "It's only space that separates us."[7]

ENLISTED MEN

In the German army in World War I, boys had to be eighteen years old to fight. But many younger boys secretly **enlisted**, or signed up, earlier—some as young as fifteen.

A typical day for a new soldier, fresh from home, would look like this:

5:30 a.m.: wake up, tidy up
6:30 a.m.: march for an hour and a half
8:00 a.m.: breakfast, then drilling and marching
12:15 p.m.: lunch
2:00 p.m. to 4:15 p.m.: more drilling and marching
4:15 p.m. and after: clean, shine boots, do special tasks

The soldiers would then learn specialized skills, such as shooting, mechanics, or radio work before going on to fight in the ground forces, or **infantry**. There were over eleven million soldiers in the German army during World War I. By the end of the war, more than half of them were either killed or wounded or missing.[8]

WALTER

Walter was injured by an exploding shell on April 23, just two weeks after leaving home. The doctors hadn't thought the wounds were serious and wrote the family to tell them not to worry. But an infection developed, and his condition worsened. From his sickbed, Walter sent a letter to his parents:

> My dears, . . . I am using my technique of thinking of other things so as not to think of the pain. There are more interesting things in the world just now than my wounds. . . . I think of you with longing, my dears, every minute of the long days and nights.
>
> From so far away,
your Walter.[9]

He died three hours later.

Walter's death changed everything. Sabine wrote:

> I can still remember that bright morning in May and the terrible shadow which suddenly blotted it out for us. . . . [W]hen a messenger brought us two telegrams I remained standing in the hall. I saw my father hastily open the envelopes, turn terribly white, go into his study and sink into the chair at his desk where he sat bowed over it with his head resting on both his arms, his face hidden in his hands.[10]

Later, the family received other letters that Walter had written in the few days before his death, saying how he had hoped they might visit. His father never stopped wishing they had.

Walter's death was a turning point for Dietrich. War had ripped apart his family. The first hymn at Walter's funeral service was "Jerusalem, Thou City Fair and High." Dietrich sang loudly and clearly, as his mother always wanted the family to do. And she did, too, drawing strength from the song's words, which spoke of God's promise to "wipe away every tear."

Dietrich's other brother Karl-Friedrich continued to fight in the army. The terrible but very real possibility that they might lose him, too, only added to his mother's heartbreak. Then her seventeen-year-old son Klaus was called up to join the army. It was too much. Paula collapsed. For several weeks, she stayed with neighbors, unable to get out of bed.

GERMANY LOSES THE WAR

In November of 1918, everything changed yet again: *Germany lost the war.*

The confusion that followed was unlike anything Germany had ever seen before. Just a few months earlier, they had been on the verge of victory. What had happened? Many blamed the **Communists**—those people who believed that all property should belong to the government and that the wealth of a country should be equally shared by all of its people. There were rumors that the Communists had spread confusion within the army. Many said they had turned the soldiers against their own government and had "stabbed it in the back." People were outraged and threatened violence in the streets.

The threat of riots, revolutions, and general chaos drove Germany to a hard decision: the **kaiser**, Germany's emperor, had to go. A new government would be formed. This government would be democratic; it would be elected by the people.

A TREATY, BUT NO PEACE

On November 9, the kaiser saw that he had no choice and resigned from the throne. In a moment, the government of old Germany vanished. But there was not a new government to replace it yet. The mobs hanging around Berlin weren't satisfied. Revolution was in the air. Angry crowds shouted for change, demanding something, *anything*—and that's just what they got. With very little thought or planning, the new German republic was born.

Jose Ignacio Soto/Shutterstock.com

The Hall of Mirrors, where the Treaty of Versailles was signed

Then, in the spring of 1919, the most humiliating and crushing blow of all came to Germany. That May, the Allies published the **Treaty of Versailles**—a peace agreement to end the Great War. The treaty was signed in the famous Hall of Mirrors at the palace of Versailles in France, but the beautiful surroundings didn't make the treaty any less ugly for the Germans. The demands listed in the treaty shocked the German people. They had thought the worst was over, but they were wrong.

The treaty required Germany to give up lands in France, Belgium, and Denmark, as well as all the Asian and African colonies it had claimed for its own. It also required Germany to pay for war damages, using all their gold, ships, lumber, coal, and livestock. But worst of all were the treaty's three biggest demands: First, Germany must give up most of its land in what is now Poland. Second, Germany must officially accept complete responsibility for causing the war. And third, Germany must slash its military down to almost nothing, leaving it with practically no army.

A FITTING PUNISHMENT?

Why were the Germans being punished? Did they start World War I? The story is more complicated than you might imagine.

It all began in 1914, in Sarajevo, Bosnia. It was like a line of dominoes falling one by one:

→ Austro-Hungary and Germany (allies) attack Serbia.
← Serbia and their allies, the Russians, defend Serbia.
← France and Russia (allies) attack Germany.
→ Germany invades Belgium as a shortcut to France.
← Britain, along with France and Belgium, declare war on Germany.
← Japan, along with France, Belgium, and Britain declare war on Germany.
← The United States declares war on Germany in 1917.

The Great War, or World War I, ended in 1918. Many felt Germany was to blame for starting the war. The Treaty of Versailles was written to punish the German people.[11]

The outcry from all parts of Germany was great. These demands were too much. They would be a death sentence for the German nation. But the people had no choice. They had to accept the treaty and the deep humiliation that came with it. The Bonhoeffer family, like all German families, followed the events closely. Living in the capitol city of Berlin, they could not avoid it.

The loss of the war and the hardships from the Treaty of Versailles created a Germany that would allow Hitler to swoop in and take over with his promises to save the nation.

DIETRICH CHOOSES THEOLOGY

At fourteen, Dietrich and Sabine were signed up for a confirmation class at the local church. In this class, they learned about the church's beliefs and teachings. When Dietrich was confirmed as a member of the church in March 1921, Paula Bonhoeffer gave him his brother Walter's Bible. For the rest of his life, he used it for his daily devotions.

Dietrich decided that he wanted to become a theologian and spend his life studying and teaching about God. It took a bold and courageous person to announce such a thing in the Bonhoeffer family. His father might treat it with respect, but his brothers and sisters and their friends would not. Klaus had chosen to study law, and Karl-Friedrich was already considered a brilliant scientist. He felt Dietrich was turning his back on scientific reality. To this, Dietrich answered, "Even if you were to knock my head off, God would still exist."

Why do some people choose to study theology? One reason might be to avoid "sloppy thinking" about religion. Sloppy thinking could mean:

- giving reasons for one's beliefs that don't make sense, either out of laziness or a lack of knowledge
- misunderstanding what the Bible actually means, and even giving others bad information based on that misunderstanding

Theologians, like Dietrich Bonhoeffer, try to seek out the truth of the Bible. Then they spread the good news about that truth as much as they can through teaching, writing, and sometimes preaching in a church.

Dietrich's decision to become a theologian stayed firm. His parents, however, weren't quite convinced this was the best path for him. He was so talented as a pianist and musician that they thought he still might turn in that direction. But later that year, Dietrich chose to take Hebrew, one of the languages he would later need to study the beginnings of the Bible.

In November 1921, at age fifteen, Bonhoeffer went to the first evangelistic meeting of his life. In these gatherings, a speaker would share the good news about Christ's forgiveness and love to people who had not yet heard of him. Thousands showed up to hear this particular **evangelist**, including many soldiers who had been broken down by the war. Sabine recalled that "Dietrich was eager to take part in it. He was the youngest person there, but he was very interested. He was impressed by the joy he had seen on [the evangelist's] face, and he told us of the people carried away by [him], and of the conversions."[12]

THINK ABOUT IT

Bonhoeffer knew at a very young age what his interests were. Write down five things you're interested in and good at. What can you dream of doing with those interests?

I'm good at . . .	I might want to be a/an . . .
Example: drawing, thinking clearly, and asking questions	architect, decorator, engineer, designer, theologian, lawyer, philosopher
1.	
2.	
3.	
4.	
5.	

CHAPTER 3

OFF TO UNIVERSITY

1923–1927

The church is only the church when it exists for others.

—DIETRICH BONHOEFFER, FROM *LETTERS AND PAPERS IN PRISON*

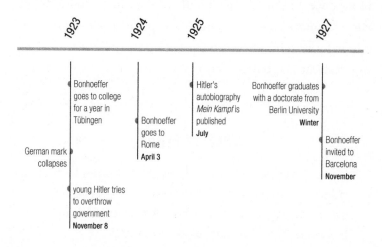

1923 **1924** **1925** **1927**

German mark collapses

Bonhoeffer goes to college for a year in Tübingen

young Hitler tries to overthrow government
November 8

Bonhoeffer goes to Rome
April 3

Hitler's autobiography *Mein Kampf* is published
July

Bonhoeffer graduates with a doctorate from Berlin University
Winter

Bonhoeffer invited to Barcelona
November

It was family tradition that all Bonhoeffers begin their university studies with a year in Tübingen, a historic university in the southeast of Germany. In 1923, it was Dietrich's turn to go. His sister, Christine, was already there. Their grandmother lived in the city, and the seventeen-year-old Dietrich and his sister stayed with her for most of their time there.

For Germany, the year 1923 was a terrible one. German money, called the **mark**, was becoming more and more worthless. In 1921, it took more than 75 German marks to make just one American dollar. The next year it took 400, and by early 1923, it took more than 7,000 German marks to equal one American dollar. The German government could not keep up with the war payments that the Treaty of Versailles demanded. Germany was bankrupt.

In October 1923, Dietrich wrote that every meal cost one billion marks. He wanted to pay for two or three weeks of meals in advance, but needed the family to send him funds. "I don't have that much money on hand," he explained. "I had to spend 6 billion for bread."[1] By November 1923, one American dollar was worth about four billion German marks.

A PRETTY PENNY

In 1923, food didn't cost as much as it does today—at least it didn't in America. But in Germany, where the Bonhoeffer family did their grocery shopping, food was so expensive that people had trouble buying what they needed. Just compare these prices.

Grocery Prices in Early 1923

PRODUCT	USA	GERMANY
Corn Flakes	10 cents a package	700 German marks
Box of Macaroni	20 cents	1,400 German marks
Loaf of Bread	9 cents	630 German marks
12 Oranges	50 cents	3,500 German marks[2]

Kondor83/Shutterstock.com

Meanwhile, on November 8, a young political activist named Adolf Hitler was put in jail for leading an effort to overthrow the government. There Hitler wrote his manifesto *Mein Kampf*—or *My Struggle*—a book full of rage, which was exactly what some suffering Germans wanted to hear. While he waited in prison, Hitler planned his next move.

manifesto

(ma-nə-ˈfes-tō) : a public declaration of intentions, opinions, obejectives, or motives.[3]

WHAT IS THE CHURCH?

When Dietrich was eighteen, he was given the chance to fulfill one of his dreams: to go to Rome, Italy. Dietrich seemed almost to have lost his mind with joy at the idea. The day after their birthday, he wrote his twin sister, Sabine, to tell her about it.

Just think, it is possible that next semester—I will be studying in Rome!! Of course, nothing is at all certain yet, but it would be absolutely the most fabulous thing that could happen to me. I can't even begin to imagine how great that would be!... [Y]ou can certainly shower me with advice; but don't be too envious while you are doing it. I'm already making inquiries everywhere around here. Everyone is telling me that it is very inexpensive. Papa still thinks that I really should postpone it. Nevertheless after thinking about it, I want to do it so much that I can't imagine ever wanting to do it more than I do now.... Talk about it a lot at home; it can only help things. Keep your ears open as well.... Best wishes, and don't be too envious.

Yours, Dietrich[4]

At last, his parents approved of the trip. On the evening of April 3, half wild with excitement, Dietrich and his brother Klaus boarded the night train for Rome. What Dietrich would do in that glorious and storied city would be more important to his future than even he expected.

The eighteen-year-old traveler kept a detailed journal. On the train, he wrote, "It feels strange when one first crosses the Italian border. Fantasy begins to transform itself into reality. Will it really be nice to have all one's wishes fulfilled? Or might I return home completely [disappointed] after all?"[5] Bonhoeffer spun through Rome like a tornado, absorbing as much of its culture as possible.

At the Vatican, the home of the pope and the capital of the Catholic church, Dietrich was overcome with the beauty of Michelangelo's paintings on the ceiling of the Sistine Chapel. In his diary, he wrote, "I am beginning, I believe, to understand the concept of 'church.'"[6] This new idea forming in the eighteen-year-old's mind that day in Rome would greatly affect the rest of his life. To think of the church as something universal—something bigger than any one country or people—would change everything for him. If the church was something that actually did exist, then it must exist not just in Germany or Rome but all over the world in many denominations.

Bonhoeffer spent a great deal of time thinking about the church during his later life. What he began to understand in Rome, he wrote about beautifully in a collection called *Letters and Papers from Prison.*

"The church is the church only when it exists for others. . . . The church must share in the . . . problems of ordinary human life, not dominating, but helping and serving. It must tell men of every calling what it means to live in Christ, to exist for others."[7]

Bonhoeffer typically threw himself into being in a new place. Throughout the week of Easter, he attended morning and afternoon Catholic Masses at some of the most beautiful churches in Rome. At every service, he used the church's pew book to follow along, studying it carefully. He had been raised in the Lutheran tradition, which is a form of Protestant faith, and the Catholic

Masses were very different from what he was used to. He wrote his parents, "The generally dreadful [reading] of these texts by the priest and the choir at home leads one to believe that the quality of the texts themselves is equally poor. This is completely wrong. For the most part the texts are wonderfully poetic and [clear]."[8]

KARL BARTH: A THEOLOGICAL ROLE MODEL

Bonhoeffer returned from Rome in mid-June and signed up to attend Berlin University. His twin sister Sabine was studying near their old hometown in Breslau and was engaged to a young lawyer named **Gerhard Leibholz**, who was Jewish. It was through Sabine and her future family that the Bonhoeffers would experience the difficulties of the years ahead in a personal way.

Bonhoeffer's main reason for choosing Berlin University was its theological professors, who were world-renowned. But there was one professor in particular—who was not in Berlin at all—who had a greater influence on Bonhoeffer than any of the others. Dietrich would admire and respect him as much as anyone else in his lifetime. He would even become a mentor and a friend. His name was **Karl Barth**.

Barth was the most important theologian of the century— many would say of the last *five* centuries. At that time, it was common for many German theology professors to teach that God might not even exist! Barth, however, declared that God actually *does* exist. His approach came to be called **neo-orthodoxy**. "Neo" means new, and "orthodoxy" refers to the traditional way of practicing the Christian faith, which follows the Bible very closely. All Bible study, he said, must be based upon the belief that God exists and that the Bible is true.

Bonhoeffer agreed with Barth. He saw the Bible as more than just a collection of historical books or writing samples. Instead, he saw the Bible as true, and the very basis of our faith.

TAUGHT BY THE BEST

Bonhoeffer looked up to Karl Barth as a role model and a great thinker. Here are some of Barth's words of wisdom on theology:

- "Prayer without study would be empty. Study without prayer would be blind."
- "Theology is not a private subject for theologians only. Nor is it a private subject for professors. . . . Nor is theology a private subject of study for pastors. . . . Theology is a matter for the Church."
- "In the Church of Jesus Christ there can and should be no non-theologians."[9]

Bonhoeffer had a massive workload during these three years at the university in Berlin. Because he was a theology student, he had to work in a local church as well as keep up with his studies. Dietrich put in more time at the church than was required, volunteering to teach a Sunday school class. Bonhoeffer became so deeply involved in this class that it took up many hours each week. He also became so popular that students from other classes left to join his class, which caused some embarrassment among the other teachers.

Out of this Sunday school class grew the Thursday Circle, a weekly reading and discussion group for young men. Bonhoeffer hand-picked each teenaged member. The group met at his home, where he taught them and led their discussions about religion and its place in the world.

Meeting once a week with a group can be great fun and great for your faith. Bonhoeffer's group talked about many things, from opera to Islam—though they made sure to tie all their discussions back to God. Some things they discussed included:

- "Did God create the world?"
- "What is the purpose of prayer?"
- "Who is Jesus Christ?"
- "Is there such a thing as a necessary lie?"

What are some things you might want to talk about in such a group?

Bonhoeffer began to wonder whether he ought to be a pastor rather than a scholar. His father and brothers thought if he went that route it would be a waste of his great mind. But Bonhoeffer often said that if you couldn't explain the deepest ideas about God and the Bible to children, something was wrong. There was more to life than university studies.

A YEAR IN BARCELONA

Bonhoeffer finished his doctoral degree and graduated from the university with honors. He was now ready for ministry training by his local church. But he was still deciding whether to become a pastor with a church or a professor and continue his studies. His family hoped he would continue his studies, but when Dietrich was offered a job with a German church in Barcelona, Spain, for one year, he decided to take it.

On the evening Dietrich was to leave, soon after his twenty-second birthday, there was a grand farewell dinner with the whole family. Everyone was there: his parents, his grandmother, and all his siblings. When the family gathering neared an end, two cabs were called. With much sadness, he said good-bye to his grandmother. Then Dietrich and the rest of the family piled into the two taxis and drove to the train station. At eleven o'clock the whistle blew, and the train pulled away. For the first time, Dietrich Bonhoeffer was truly on his own. For the next year he would be away from family. And for the first time since he could remember, he would not be a student. Dietrich had set off into the wide world.

THINK ABOUT IT

1. How do you feel about reading the Bible? Could God be revealing himself to you through his Word?
2. How could you begin—right now—to be a theologian? What questions about God would you ask?
3. Bonhoeffer said that "the church is the church only when it exists for others"—that it should help and serve others, and lead others to know Christ. List some ways your church shows the love of Christ in your community. What other things could your church do?

CHAPTER 4

VENTURING ABROAD

1928–1930

God does not love some ideal person, but rather human beings just as we are, not some ideal world, but rather the real world.

—DIETRICH BONHOEFFER

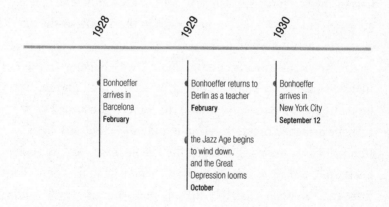

1928	1929	1930
Bonhoeffer arrives in Barcelona **February**	Bonhoeffer returns to Berlin as a teacher **February**	Bonhoeffer arrives in New York City **September 12**
	the Jazz Age begins to wind down, and the Great Depression looms **October**	

Bonhoeffer was met at the train station in Barcelona, Spain, by the German pastor who would be his boss, a "large, dark-haired . . . man" who "looks quite unlike a pastor, but is not elegant."[1] The pastor brought his new assistant to the creaky, rather primitive boardinghouse that would be his home. There was only one place for everyone to wash up. Dietrich's brother Karl-Friedrich, who visited later, described it as "very like a third-class lavatory on a train, except that it doesn't shake."[2] The three women who ran the boardinghouse spoke only Spanish. They did their best to pronounce his name, "Dietrich." They failed.

In Barcelona, Bonhoeffer discovered a world strikingly different from Berlin. The German community there was made up of serious and conservative people. They seemed to be untouched by the dramatic events of the last ten years in Germany. There was nothing in Barcelona like the intellectual community Bonhoeffer had so enjoyed in Berlin. Dietrich was amazed at how people of all ages seemed to sit for hours in cafés in the middle of the day, chattering about meaningless things.

There was, however, one activity Dietrich enjoyed there that he could never enjoy in Berlin: watching bullfighting. But he had gone to Barcelona mainly to serve the church. While there he preached nineteen sermons and ran a children's service. Bonhoeffer's sermons challenged the people there, both in their hearts and in their minds. In his first sermon, he spoke about the difference between a faith based on what we ourselves do and one based on what God does for us—grace. Soon, the crowds for Dietrich's sermons became much larger than those of the other pastors. Dietrich's boss quickly stopped announcing who would be preaching so that people would come to all the services.

In his letters home, Bonhoeffer wrote that the older pastor, his boss, had "done nothing in the way of addressing the younger generation."[3] Only some of the children were being taught in classes, so Bonhoeffer asked to start classes for the rest of the children. Every time the older pastor turned around, Bonhoeffer was wanting to start something that would make more work for him when the young assistant left. So the older pastor axed the idea.

Bonhoeffer's parents visited him in Barcelona in September. They heard their son preach on a topic that was important to him throughout his life: "God wants to see human beings," he said, "not ghosts who shun the world." He said that in "the whole of human history" only the present day is important. God's people must live out their faith by serving others in the times in which they live.[4]

BLOOM WHERE YOU'RE PLANTED

Do you ever feel like someone is shooting down every idea you have? Like you and your dreams don't fit into the world around you? It might have seemed that way for Dietrich, when he tried to improve the church in Barcelona. But when that happened, he had two options:

1. wither (whine, complain, give up, and feel sorry for himself)
   or
2. bloom (keep giving his best effort; keep thinking of new and better ways to serve, and store up his ideas for the future)

Bonhoeffer could have chosen to give up and wither. Instead, he chose to bloom where he was planted, until God moved him on to a bigger pot—a place where his ideas could grow even bigger. Is there a place in your life where you're tempted to wither? How can you choose to bloom instead?

Bonhoeffer continued to teach through the fall of 1928. In November, he was asked to stay in Barcelona, but he wasn't quite sure what he wanted to do. He had enjoyed his year in Spain and was considering joining the ministry full time. But at twenty-three, he was two years too young to become a pastor officially. He would have to wait until he was at least twenty-five. Dietrich decided to spend those two years of waiting as a teacher at Berlin University.

BACK IN BERLIN

Bonhoeffer returned to Berlin from Spain in February 1929. But the Germany he returned to was becoming more and more impatient with the new government formed after World War I. The country missed having its kaiser (or emperor), and people thought the new parliamentary system of government was a disorganized disaster. No one political party seemed to have the power to lead. And for many, the endless arguing of the new system was simply un-German. Many longed for a return to some kind of strong leadership. But the people were growing less and less fussy about what kind of leadership that should be. It was the perfect time for Hitler and the Nazis to begin their grab for power.

BEST FRIENDS IN BERLIN

In Berlin, Bonhoeffer struck up a friendship with a wisecracking theology student named **Franz Hildebrandt**. Hildebrandt became Bonhoeffer's best friend, his first close friend outside the family. In a few years he would also become Bonhoeffer's closest ally in the church's struggle against the Nazis. Hildebrandt had grown up in the same district of Berlin where the Bonhoeffers had lived. His father was a famous historian, and his mother was Jewish. By Nazi standards at that time, this made him a Jew— even though Franz himself was a Christian.

Many people with Jewish ancestors in Germany—like Sabine's husband, Gerhard—were baptized Christians. And many of them, like Franz Hildebrandt, were so serious about their Christian faith that they chose to enter the ministry as their life's work. Franz himself was going to be a pastor of a Christian church. But in just a few short years, as part of their efforts to push Jews out of Germany, the Nazis would attempt to push anyone with a Jewish background out of the German church too. The fact that people had become Christians meant nothing to the Nazis.

A TRIP TO AMERICA

While in Berlin as a teacher in 1929, the twenty-four-year-old Bonhoeffer continued his study of theology. More than ever, Bonhoeffer began to see the importance of being able to speak the truth out loud. When talking about one of his favorite professors, he declared:

> It became clear to us through him that truth is born only of freedom. We saw in him the champion of the free expression of a truth once recognized . . . despite the fear-ridden restraint of the majority. This made him . . . the friend of all young people who spoke their opinions freely.[5]

Dietrich's work had qualified him as a university teacher, just as he had planned. But soon, he began thinking about going to America for another year of study. His advisor recommended it, since he was still too young to be a pastor of his own church. The decision to go to America would change his life.

BRIGHT LIGHTS, BIG CITY

On September 14, 1930, two days after Bonhoeffer's arrival in America, an election was held in Germany, and the results were shocking. The Nazis had entered the race as the smallest of Germany's political parties, with only a pitiful twelve members in the government. By day's end they had done better than even Hitler had dreamed. They gained 107 seats and became the second largest political party in the land.

But in America, Bonhoeffer knew nothing about the election. New York City at the end of the **Jazz Age** was a dizzying place for any visitor, even one as cultured and sophisticated as Dietrich Bonhoeffer. If Berlin was seen as the beautiful, but weary actress just past her prime, New York City was the crazy, energetic, bright-eyed teenage starlet in full growth spurt. The whole island seemed to be bursting at the seams in every direction—and grinning as it did so.

THE JAZZ AGE

Bonhoeffer reached New York at the very end of the "Jazz Age." America had been booming for years, when it seemed like everyone had big money to spend and big dreams to dream. But on

October 29, 1929, that would all begin to crumble as the stock market collapsed, sending America into the Great Depression. Still, Bonhoeffer was able to see New York in the last part of its full, jazzy swing. In the Jazz Age:

- America's wealth more than doubled.
- Jazz music first came on the scene, as did "flappers" and old-time gangsters like Al Capone.
- Women were given the right to vote (1920).
- A Ford Model T car cost just $260 (1924).
- Inventions like the electric refrigerator, the washing machine, and vacuum cleaners made life easier, while affordable radios connected the nation like never before.
- One of the first "talkie" movies was released, called *The Jazz Singer* (1927).
- Mickey Mouse was created (1928).
- Words such as *dough* (money), *hip* (trendy), *swanky* (elegant), and *lollygagger* (a lazy person) made their way into the American language.[6]

"THERE IS NO THEOLOGY HERE . . ."

Despite the lively surroundings, Bonhoeffer arrived at the Union Theological Seminary in New York with a bit of a chip on his shoulder and not without reason. Bonhoeffer had a doctorate from Berlin University and could easily have taught at Union instead of studying there. German theologians were the best in the world, and he had studied with the best of the best. Yet Dietrich found the educational situation at Union even worse than he had feared. In a letter to his old academic advisor, he wrote:

> There is no theology here. . . . They talk a blue streak without the slightest . . . foundation and with no evidence. . . . The students—on the average twenty-five to thirty years old—are completely clueless. . . . They are unfamiliar with even the most basic questions.[7]

In spite of his doubts about the quality of the education, Bonhoeffer did see that American theological students knew more about "everyday matters" than German students did. The Americans were more focused on how theology was applied to practical life and "social needs" than to "preparation for the ministry."

Dietrich saw that one group of students had "over the winter, continually provided food and lodging for thirty unemployed—among them three Germans—and has advised them as well as possible." While he appreciated these good deeds, he still felt that this group of American students had almost no theological education.[8]

THE BIG QUESTIONS

Theology is meant to ask big questions and seek answers from God, history, and the Bible. These big questions don't usually have short answers, but they're some of the most important ones you can ask in your life. What answers can you find in the Bible to the following questions?

- How can I know what God is like?
- Who has God made us to be?
- What are God's plans for the world?
- How does God save his people? Why does he love us?
- What will happen when the world ends?

You don't have to be a university professor to explore the world of theology. You just need an open mind, big questions, and a heart that's hungry for the truth.[9]

Still another group of students was mostly interested in the philosophy of religion—the study of ideas, truth, and meaning in religion. But Bonhoeffer said that "the lack of seriousness with which the students here speak of God and the world is, to say the least, extremely surprising."[10]

His conclusion was withering: "I am in fact of the opinion that one can learn extraordinarily little over there."[11] But he soon found that there was more to learn from America than he had expected.

As always, Bonhoeffer did much more than focus on school. He wasted no time in exploring the city and all it had to offer, and he did most of it with a small group of fellow Union students. One of these close friends was **Albert Franklin "Frank" Fisher**, an African-American student who grew up in Alabama. Their friendship would turn out to have the greatest influence of all on Dietrich during his time in America.

THINK ABOUT IT

1. Why was Bonhoeffer so irritated at the American theology school? What were they missing?
2. The American school was doing something right though. What were the American students doing that the German students were missing?
3. Why is it wrong to just study the Bible and not act on its teachings?
4. Why is it wrong to act—to just follow orders—without thinking about why you are doing what you are doing?
5. What was the danger the Germans faced by not asking *why* their leaders were doing the things they were doing?

CHAPTER 5

A NEW WAY OF SEEING THE CHURCH

1930–1933

We must be ready to allow ourselves to be interrupted by God.

—DIETRICH BONHOEFFER

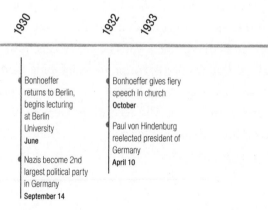

1930 · 1932 · 1933

Bonhoeffer
returns to Berlin,
begins lecturing
at Berlin
University
June

Nazis become 2nd
largest political party
in Germany
September 14

Bonhoeffer gives fiery
speech in church
October

Paul von Hindenburg
reelected president of
Germany
April 10

Bonhoeffer had been less than impressed by American churches, especially in New York City. The one exception was in what was known as the "negro churches," whose members were almost entirely African Americans. If Dietrich's year in New York had value, it was mainly because of his experiences in these "negro churches."

When his friend Frank Fisher invited Bonhoeffer to one of those church services, he was thrilled to go along. There, in the socially downtrodden African-American community of Harlem in the 1930s, Bonhoeffer would finally hear the real gospel of Jesus Christ preached and would clearly see its power. He witnessed people being truly joyful about what Jesus had done for them in their lives.

The preacher at Frank's church was a powerful speaker who easily held the attention of the church's fourteen thousand members. In fact, the church was probably the largest Protestant church of any kind in the whole United States. When Bonhoeffer saw it all, he was amazed.

Bonhoeffer searched New York record shops to find recordings of the "negro spirituals" that had so moved him on those Sundays in Harlem. The joyous power of this music convinced him of the importance of music in worshiping God. He would later take these recordings back to Germany and play them for his students in Berlin. The recordings were some of his most treasured belongings, and for many of his students, they seemed as exotic as moon rocks.

SPIRITUALS FOR SUFFERING: "GO DOWN, MOSES"

Some of the most famous African-American spirituals talk about looking to God for help in times of pain and cruelty. When black Americans were suffering under slavery in America, their songs were not only cries to God for help, but also reminders of his love for them. One of these songs, "Go Down, Moses," talks about the slavery of the Jews under the Egyptians. Moses led the Jews to freedom, with miracles from God all along the way. Little did Bonhoeffer know that the Jews were about to be crushed again—this time by the Nazis. Nor did he know that he would be part of God's plan to free the Jews from the evils of Hitler and his madmen. Though it is well over 150 years old, "Go Down, Moses" is still a comfort to those who are suffering.

When Israel was in Egypt's land,
let my people go;
oppressed so hard they could
  not stand,
let my people go.

Refrain:
Go down, (go down) Moses,
  (Moses)
way down in Egypt's land;
tell old Pharaoh
to let my people go!

This world's a wilderness of
  woe,
let my people go;
O let us on to Canaan go,
let my people go.

(Refrain)

O let us all from bondage flee,
let my people go;
and let us all in Christ be free,
let my people go.

(Refrain)

Bonhoeffer became deeply interested in the racial issue in America. By 1930, slavery had been outlawed for almost sixty-five years, but black Americans still fought against prejudice and injustice. To his brother Karl-Friedrich, Dietrich wrote:

> I want to have a look at church conditions in the South . . . and get to know the situation of the Negroes in a bit more detail. . . . We don't really have a [similar] situation in Germany, but I've just found it enormously interesting, and I've never for a moment found it boring. And it really does seem to me that there is a real movement forming, and I do believe that the negroes will still give the whites here considerably more than merely their folk-songs.[1]

Unfortunately, Bonhoeffer's belief that there was no similar situation in Germany would change soon enough, when he found out what the Nazis were doing to the Jews. Like his younger brother, Karl-Friedrich didn't see a similar situation in Germany at that time. He even said, "Our Jewish question is a joke by comparison; there won't be many people who claim they are oppressed here."[2] He was soon to learn just how horribly wrong he was.

A FIERY SPEECH

Bonhoeffer returned to Berlin from America at the end of June 1931, a few months after turning twenty-five. He had been in New York just nine months, but in some ways it seemed a lifetime. He was at last old enough to be ordained as a minister.

Bonhoeffer was asked to preach at a local church in Berlin

on Reformation Sunday in 1932. This was the day Germany celebrated the period of church history known as the **Reformation**. It was during the Reformation that a radical German priest named **Martin Luther** started a split from the Catholic church and demanded "reform" from the injustices he saw in the church. That was the beginning of the Protestant church. The German people took great pride in their "Lutheran" legacy. The people sitting in the pews that Reformation Sunday expected about what an American might expect from a July 4th service in an American church: an uplifting, patriotic sermon. They expected to be filled with pride at the miracle of their German Lutheran tradition. They also expected to be congratulated for keeping this grand tradition alive by coming to church and sitting in the hard pews. After all, there were so many other things they could have been doing.

Thus the sermon that Bonhoeffer delivered that day must have seemed like a tremendous shock.

Bonhoeffer began with bad news: the Protestant church was on its last legs, he said, and it's "high time we realized this."[3] The German church, he said, is dying or is already dead. What he had seen in America—particularly in the African-American churches—had convinced him that a living church was a place of joy and bravery. It was not a place where people went to pat themselves on the back for simply showing up. The fiery sermons and the lively, exuberant worship and singing in Harlem had opened Bonhoeffer's eyes and changed him. He now condemned the thought of having a celebration when they were all, in fact, attending a funeral. He then referred to the day's hero, Martin Luther, as a "dead man" whom they were propping up for their selfish purposes. It was as if he'd first thrown a bucket of water on the congregation and had then thrown his shoes at them.

For the first time in his life, Bonhoeffer became a regular churchgoer and took Communion as often as possible. When friends visited Berlin in 1933, they noticed a difference in him immediately. He had always loved discussing theological *ideas*— but now there was something new. Clearly something had happened to Bonhoeffer in America—and was happening still.

A TALENTED TEACHER

In 1933, Bonhoeffer took a teaching job at Berlin University. But the change that had been occurring in him was visible in the classroom too. Everywhere he went, it seemed, crowds of young people gathered around him, hungry to learn. One of his students remembered what he was like as a teacher:

A young lecturer stepped to the [front] with a light, quick step, a man with very fair, rather thin hair, a broad face, rimless glasses with a golden bridge. After a few words of welcome he explained the meaning and structure of the lecture, in a firm, slightly throaty way of speaking. Then he opened his manuscript and started on his lecture. He pointed out that nowadays we often ask ourselves whether we still need the Church, whether we still need God. But this question, he said, is wrong. We are the ones who are questioned. The Church exists and God exists, and we are asked whether we are willing to be of service, for God needs us.[4]

Art Resource

Bonhoeffer with some of his younger students

Talk like this was rare in most German churches. In a university it was simply unheard of. Another student said they "followed his words with such close attention that one could hear the flies humming. Sometimes, when we laid our pens down after a lecture, we were literally [sweating]."[5] Still another student remembered her first lecture with Bonhoeffer:

My first impression of him was that he was so young! . . . He had a good face, and he had good posture. . . . He was very natural with us students . . . but there was, for such a young man, a certainty and dignity in him. . . . He always maintained a certain distance. . . . One wouldn't have trusted oneself to make a joke around him.[6]

A group of students formed around him during this time. Their conversations overflowed out of the classrooms and into to homes and restaurants. It was no aimless chattering, but a controlled and serious exploration of questions. The students learned how to take the time to think things through to the end.

One of his students remembered that on one evening Bonhoeffer brought along the records of "negro spirituals" he had bought in New York:

> He told us of his colored friend with whom he had travelled through the States . . . he told of the piety of the negroes. . . . At the end of the evening he said: "When I took leave of my black friend, he said to me: 'Make our sufferings known in Germany, tell them what is happening to us, and show them what we are like.' I wanted to [do this] tonight."[7]

Bonhoeffer's interest was not only in teaching his students as a university lecturer. He wished to "disciple" them in the true life of the Christian. This approach was very different from what usually happened in German university theology programs of that time.

MODERN-DAY DISCIPLES

Jesus' twelve disciples aren't the last disciples who ever lived. In fact, anyone who studies and follows Jesus' ways can become a disciple. To *disciple* someone, as Bonhoeffer did, is to teach them how to live as a Christian. "Discipleship" training usually includes learning:

- how to study the Bible and what it says about important topics
- how to be part of a church community
- how to pray
- what to do about sin, and what to do when you are wrong
- how to solve common problems
- how God is with you in your everyday life
- how to serve God and follow the plan he has for your life

Most churches have youth pastors whose job is to disciple young people. Ask your pastor, parents, or youth pastor how you can become a disciple too.

One of Bonhoeffer's students said, "Among the public, there spread the expectation that the salvation of the German people would now come from Hitler. But in Bonhoeffer's lectures we were told that salvation comes only from Jesus Christ."[8] Hitler's supporters were expected to say, *"Heil, Hitler!"* ("Hail, Hitler!") to show respect for his authority over them. But Bonhoeffer warned his students about saying, *"Heil!"* to anyone but God. He didn't back away from political issues. From the beginning he never felt that he could be true to his Christian faith and still support the Nazis—though sadly many others did.

In August, four generations of Bonhoeffers gathered together to celebrate Dietrich's grandmother's ninetieth birthday. His family could not help noticing the change that had taken place in him since he left for New York. But the change was not an awkward, embarrassing phase that he would later regret; rather, it was a deepening of his beliefs. In light of all this, his faith—like the faith of his mother—was difficult to argue with, no matter how much one might have wanted to do so.

THINK ABOUT IT

1. What did Bonhoeffer learn from the African-American community that might give hope to the Jews in Nazi Germany?
2. Why do you think Bonhoeffer cared so much about teaching young people?
3. Have you ever thought of yourself as a disciple? Write down the names of a few adults who could "disciple" you—and then ask one of them to do it.
4. Has someone ever told you a hard truth that seemed like a tremendous shock? Was it when your parents disciplined you? When a teacher corrected your work? How can such a "shock" be good for you?

CHAPTER 6

NAZI LIES

1933

It's been our misfortune to have the wrong religion. . . . Why did it have to be Christianity with its meekness and flabbiness?

—ADOLF HITLER

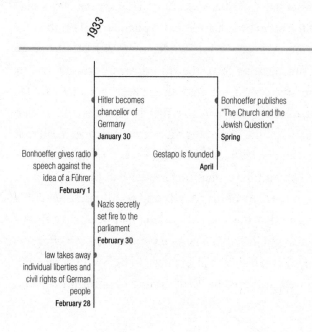

1933

Hitler becomes
chancellor of
Germany
January 30

Bonhoeffer publishes
"The Church and the
Jewish Question"
Spring

Bonhoeffer gives radio
speech against the
idea of a Führer
February 1

Gestapo is founded
April

Nazis secretly
set fire to the
parliament
February 30

law takes away
individual liberties and
civil rights of German
people
February 28

At noon on January 30, 1933, Adolf Hitler became the democratically elected chancellor of Germany. Though Germany still had a president, **Paul von Hindenburg**, Hitler was now one of the highest government officials in the land. The Third Reich, or "Third Empire," had begun. Hitler was now the **Führer**, which means leader, of all Germany.

Two days later, on February 1, a twenty-six-year-old theologian named Dietrich Bonhoeffer gave a radio address about the deep-rooted problems of leadership by such a Führer. He explained how such a leader always becomes an idol and a "*misleader.*" But before he could finish, the speech was cut off.

This story is usually told as though Bonhoeffer had bravely put himself forward to speak out against Hitler, whose henchmen ordered the microphones turned off and the broadcast ended. But, in fact, the speech had been scheduled for some time and was not a response to Hitler's election. Though the Nazis may have cut off the radio broadcast, it's also possible that Bonhoeffer and the station manager had misunderstood each other, and he simply ran out of time. Still, the timing was uncanny. In any case, Bonhoeffer was upset that the speech ended early. He didn't want his listeners to think that he approved of Hitler. Anyone who heard the end of his speech would understand that Bonhoeffer thought the idea of a Führer was a terrible one. But since no one heard the ending, Bonhoeffer had the speech copied and sent it to many of his friends and relatives, along with a note explaining that the speech's ending had been cut off. His speech was also published in a newspaper. Then Bonhoeffer was invited to give his full speech at a college in Berlin. In early 1933, such things were still possible without fear of punishment from the Nazis.

WHAT'S WRONG WITH A FÜHRER?

Bonhoeffer's speech began by explaining why Germany was looking for a Führer—for a leader who also set himself up as a savior for the nation. The First World War had brought depression, struggle, and crisis. The younger people, especially, had lost all hope in traditional authorities like the kaiser (emperor) and the church. The German idea of the Führer came from these young people and their search for a way out of their troubles. So what was the difference between real leadership and the false leadership of the Führer? Real leadership gets its authority from God, the source of all goodness. But the Führer answered to no one but himself.

FALSE GODS

Bonhoeffer was worried that Hitler was making himself into a "false god," or what the Bible calls an "idol." In fact, when God gave Moses the Ten Commandments, the very first commandment had to do with idols:

"You must not have any other god but me. You must not make for yourself an idol of any kind or an image of anything in the heavens or on the earth or in the sea" (Exodus 20:3–4 NLT).

So what is an "idol" or a "false god"? It is:

- something or someone you love more than God
- something you worship and feel like you can't live without
- something you place all your hope in, dreaming that it will make your life so much better

---

Hitler was an "idol" for some German people because they placed all their hope in him instead of God. They thought he was the answer to all their troubles.

What kinds of "idols" do people have today?

- stuff—the things you own and want to own
- celebrities and sports stars
- self—how you look and what people think of you

If there are things crowding God out of your head and heart, then ask him to help you put them in their right place today.

Only two days had passed since Hitler's election, but with Bonhoeffer's speech the battle lines were drawn.

Hitler gave a speech that day too. He was just forty-three years old, but he had already struggled in the political wilderness half his life. Now he was the chancellor of Germany. The opening words of his speech that day were: "We are determined, as leaders of the nation, to fulfill as a national government the task which has been given to us, swearing [loyalty] only to God, our conscience, and our [people]."[1]

Hitler then declared that his government would make Christianity "the basis of our collective morality." This statement, however, was a lie. He ended with another prayer to the God he did not believe in, but whose Jewish and Christian followers he would soon begin to persecute and kill: "May God Almighty take our work into his grace!"[2]

Four weeks later, Bonhoeffer preached at the Trinity Church in Berlin. It was the first time he had preached since Hitler had come to power. Bonhoeffer saw the new situation for what it was and was not afraid to preach what he saw:

> The church has only *one* altar, the altar of the Almighty . . . before which all creatures must kneel. . . . The church has only one pulpit, and from that pulpit, faith in God will be preached, and no other faith, and no other will than the will of God, however well-intentioned.[3]

The theme was the same as in his radio address, but now everyone knew who the false god was that would be worshiped. *Now* the dangerous Führer had a name.

BURNING DOWN THE GOVERNMENT

When Hitler and the Nazis gained power on January 31, they didn't have control of the entire German government yet. There was still a president, along with other elected officials. But Hitler knew no one was organized enough to fight against him. He would seize power with breathtaking speed and cold-blooded skill for which no one was prepared. One Nazi official wrote, "Now it will be easy to carry on the fight, for we can call on all the resources of the State. Radio and press are [ours]. We shall stage a masterpiece of **propaganda**. And this time, naturally, there is no lack of money."

PROPAGANDA

The Nazi party used many forms of *propaganda* to lie to the people. Posters, movies, fliers, cartoons, and fake news stories were pumped out by the Nazi propaganda office to convince people to go along with Hitler's plans. Soon people didn't know what was true and what was a lie anymore.

Here are some slogans from Nazi propaganda posters:

Art Resource

"The German Student Fights for the Führer and the People."

But how would the Nazis "carry on the fight"? First, they would burn down a building. It was a scheme that was at once foolproof and foolish: The Nazis would start a fire at the main building of the German **parliament**. Then they would blame it on another political party, the Communists. If the German people believed the Communists had tried to burn down the parliament building, they would see the need for the government to crack down and defend the country. They would welcome giving up a few freedoms to protect the German nation from the Communist devils. So the fire was set.

The fire took even some Nazi leaders by surprise. But it served Hitler's purposes and gave him the excuse he needed to make sure that his iron grip on the country would be complete.

The very day after the fire, when the building was still smoking, Hitler visited the president of Germany, Paul von Hindenburg. Hitler convinced him that this was an emergency, and that they should put a hold on those parts of the German constitution that gave people individual freedoms and civil rights. Supposedly, that would help the police keep order. The changes were signed and put into effect before anyone had had time to think carefully about them. It was these changes that made possible most of the horrors ahead, including the **concentration camps**. These camps—located throughout Germany's captured lands—were the worst imaginable sorts of places. Jews, political prisoners, and others were sent there. Millions died in the camps—either from the forced labor, starvation, or murder.

Hitler's move limited personal freedoms, including freedom to express opinions and freedom of the press. It also took away the German people's right to privacy in letters, calls, and telegraphs. Their houses could be searched at any time, and their things could be taken for any reason.[4]

Within days, Nazi storm troopers were in the streets, arresting and beating up their political enemies, many of whom were imprisoned, tortured, and killed. But Hitler was not through. To formally and legally control the whole government, he would need to take away all power from the parliament. He claimed it was for the good of the nation, of course. He requested a new law that would put everything in the eager hands of the chancellor and the group of advisors in his cabinet. And so, on March 23, like a snake swallowing its own tail, the German parliament passed the law that wiped out its own existence.

The speed of the Nazi takeover of German society was staggering. No one dreamed how quickly and dramatically things would change.

STANDING UP FOR THE JEWS

The Bonhoeffers had always been in the know about secret information because of their important friends. But as the shadow of the Third Reich fell across Germany, much of the information came from their daughter Christine's husband, **Hans von Dohnanyi**. He was Dietrich's brother-in-law and a lawyer at the German Supreme Court. Through him the Bonhoeffers learned that something especially worrying would soon take effect. A law was about to be passed that said anyone of Jewish descent would lose his job in the government. If the German church—which was basically a government church—went along with it, all pastors with Jewish blood would be forbidden from preaching too.

Many people were confused about what to do. Dietrich knew that someone needed to think through all of this very carefully before reacting. In March 1933, he wrote an essay called "The Church and the Jewish Question." The most serious problem he wrote about was the willingness of Christian leaders to consider forcing anyone with a Jewish background out of the ministry.

Bonhoeffer reminded the Christian leaders that governments are established by God. They're put on earth for the protection of law and order. Bonhoeffer then famously listed "three possible ways in which the church can act towards the state":

1. The church could question the state about its actions and their rightness—to help the state be a good state as God has intended.
2. The church could "aid the victims of state action," or help those the government had hurt.
3. Finally, the church could act against the state to stop it from hurting its own people.[5]

BEING BRAVE

A Christian's job is more than just helping hurting people, Bonhoeffer said. It is also to stop the things that hurt them. It takes bravery to try to stop a big, crushing wheel like the Nazi government. But you can be brave, too, and stand up for people who can't stand up for themselves.

That might mean . . .

- not only being nice to a kid who is bullied, but also reporting the bully to a teacher
- not only keeping out of gossip, but also speaking up and defending the person others are gossiping about
- not only giving your spare change to a hungry person on the street, but also volunteering at a shelter or food bank

List some other acts of kindness below. How can you take kindness to the next level?

_____

_____

_____

_____

Bonhoeffer added that this last point, number 3, was what the church should do if the state forced "baptized Jews from our Christian congregations" or tried to stop the church from teaching Jews about Jesus. Telling *everyone*—including the Jews—about Jesus was the church's most important job. If Hitler's laws were adopted, this would be impossible. It was the spring of 1933, and already Bonhoeffer was declaring it the duty of the church to stand up for the Jews.

"BOYCOTT THE JEWS"

One week after taking complete control, Hitler declared a **boycott** of Jewish stores across Germany. That meant that no one was supposed to shop in any stores owned by Jews. Hitler said it was to stop the international press—which the Nazis said was controlled by the Jews—from printing lies about the Nazi regime. Everywhere across Germany, brown-shirted Nazi soldiers scared shoppers away from Jewish-owned stores. Their store windows were smeared in black or yellow paint with stars of David and the word *Jude* (Jew). The Nazis had taken a symbol beloved by Jews—the six-pointed star of David—and used it against them. The Nazi soldiers also handed out pamphlets and held up signs that said, "Germans, protect yourselves! Don't buy from Jews!" Even the offices of Jewish doctors and lawyers were targeted.

On the day of the boycott in Berlin, Dietrich's grandmother was out shopping. The feisty ninety-year-old was not about to be told where to shop. When Nazi soldiers tried to keep her from entering one store, she told them that she would shop where she liked and that is exactly what she did. Later that day she did the same thing at the famous Kaufhaus des Westens, the world's largest department store, ignoring the line of Nazi soldiers stationed in front.

Sabine's husband Gerhard—like many German Jews—was a baptized Christian. But because of Gerhard's Jewish background, Karl and Paula Bonhoeffer were worried about their daughter and son-in-law. They went to stay with Sabine and Gerhard that weekend, while other family members checked in by telephone.

anti-Semitism

(an-tē-' se-mə-ti-zəm): hatred of Jewish people

*Semite is a word that means "a member of any of a group of people from southwestern Asia, chiefly represented by the Jews and Arabs."

*Anti- comes from a Greek word that means "against."[6]

Gerhard was a popular professor of law at one of the universities, so it wasn't long before he and Sabine were directly affected by the rising tide of anti-Semitism. At one point, some student leaders at the school called for a boycott of his classes. Sabine remembered:

I had often heard my husband's lectures and I went to the university on the actual day of the boycott in order to be there and to hear what the students would have to say. A few students were standing there in [Nazi] uniform, straddling the doorway in their jackboots . . . and not allowing anyone to enter. "Leibholz must not lecture, he is a Jew. The lectures are not taking place," [they said]. Obediently the students went home.[7]

After a while, Sabine and Gerhard needed only to walk down the street in their hometown to breathe the poisonous atmosphere of anti-Semitism. People who recognized them crossed to the other side of the street to avoid them. But a few friends were sickened by what was taking place and were not afraid to express their horror. A theologian they knew met them on the street and launched into a rant against Hitler. When Gerhard eventually lost his job at the university, another professor approached him and, with tears in his eyes, said, "Sir, you are my colleague and I am ashamed to be a German."

A BONFIRE OF BOOKS

Throughout 1933, the Nazis continued their efforts to legally ban Jews from state-run institutions, such as schools, hospitals, and courts. The next few months read like a checklist of discrimination:

- April 22: Jews were banned from serving as certain types of lawyers, and Jewish doctors were forbidden from working in hospitals with state-run insurance.
- April 25: Strict limits were placed on how many Jewish children could attend public schools.
- May 6: All Jewish honorary university professors, lecturers, and notaries were banned from teaching.

- June: All Jewish dentists and dental technicians were forbidden from working within state-run institutions.
- Fall: The spouses of Jews were forbidden to work for any state-run institutions.
- September 29: Jews were banned from all cultural and entertainment activities, including the worlds of film, theater, literature, and the arts.
- October: All newspapers were placed under Nazi control, expelling Jews from the world of journalism.

Anti-Semitism had existed for decades among the students of German universities, but now they felt free to show it. That spring the German Students Association planned to celebrate an "Action against the un-German Spirit" on May 10. At 11:00 p.m. thousands of students gathered in every university town across Germany. From one end of the country to the other, they marched in torch-light parades. They were whipped into a wild-eyed frenzy as Nazi officials raved about the glories of what the brave young men and women of Germany were about to do. At midnight huge bonfires were lit. The students hurled thousands of books into the fires in a huge "cleansing." Thus Germany would be "cleansed" of the "un-German" thoughts of authors such as Helen Keller, Jack London (who wrote *White Fang*), H. G. Wells (who wrote *The Time Machine*), and even the famous physicist Albert Einstein.

In Berlin the torchlight procession began behind Berlin University, went through the university, and then moved eastward. The "anti-German" books followed in a truck. At the end of their route stood the great pile of wood that would become the bonfire. Thirty thousand students gathered to toss books into the fire while Nazi official **Joseph Goebbels** ranted: "You are doing the right thing at this midnight hour—to consign to the flames the unclean spirit of the past."[8]

Eric Metaxas photo

A plaque in Berlin on the site where thirty thousand students gathered at midnight to burn the books of "un-German" authors. On the left is a quote from the German poet Heinrich Heine: "Where books are burned, they will, in the end, burn people, too." On the right: "In the middle of this plaza on May 10, 1933 Nazi students burned the works of hundreds of authors, publishers, philosophers, and scientists."

HITLER'S HENCHMAN: JOSEPH GOEBBELS

Hitler didn't come to power all by himself. He had many clever and ruthless men who helped to carry out his plans. One of his closest henchmen was Joseph Goebbels.

Though he was not well-liked, Goebbels was an expert in propaganda, psychology, and public speaking. He could speak in a way that made people listen and agree. His title was "Minister of Propaganda" and president of the "Chamber of Culture." That put him in charge of making sure newspapers, radio, theatre, movies, news reports, books, music, and the arts all glorified Hitler and threatened the Jews. Because he was good at convincing people to think and do what Hitler wanted them to, he became one of the most important and dangerous people in the Third Reich.[9]

THE NAZI CHURCH

In 1933, Hitler never hinted that he was planning on taking a stand against the churches. Most pastors were quite convinced that Hitler was on their side, partly because he had a record of making pro-Christian statements in the press. In a 1922 speech, he called Jesus "our greatest **Aryan** hero." The Nazis chose to ignore the fact that Jesus was, of course, Jewish! In truth, Hitler really had no religion other than serving himself. He used the church when it was helpful to him, and when it wasn't, he didn't mind taking a stand against it.

Aryan

('a-rē-ən) : the term used by Nazis to describe the ideal German, someone who was fair-skinned with blonde hair and with absolutely no Jewish ancestry.

Other Nazi leaders, however, were bitterly anti-Christian and were completely opposed to the ideas of Christianity. They wanted to replace it with a religion of their own invention. Very early on, **Heinrich Himmler**, the head of an elite German military police organization called the **SS**, barred pastors and priests from serving as "soldiers" in its ranks. In 1935, he ordered every SS member to resign leadership in religious organizations. The next year he forbade SS musicians to go to religious services, even if they didn't wear their uniforms. Soon afterward he forbade SS members to attend any church services. For Himmler, the SS was itself a religion, and its members were trainees in its priesthood.

Another Nazi official outlined a program for a "new religion," or "National Church." Just a few points of his program show what Hitler was willing to approve. Later, under cover of war, Hitler would move toward making this program actual law:

- The National Church forbids the publishing, printing, selling, or distributing of the Bible.
- The National Church will clear away from its altars all crucifixes, Bibles, and pictures of saints.
- On the altars there must be nothing but Hitler's book, *Mein Kampf* (which was the most sacred book to the German nation and therefore to God). To the left of the altar should be a sword.
- On the day of the National Church's foundation, the Christian Cross must be removed from all churches, cathedrals, and chapels . . . and it must be replaced by the only unconquerable symbol, the **swastika**.[10]

THE SWASTIKA

Jim Vallee/Shutterstock.com

The Nazi symbol was called a *swastika*, which is like a cross with bent arms. It originally came from ancient India, where it stood for "prosperity and good fortune."

Goebbels (the Minister of Propaganda) and the Nazis put it everywhere, so people would constantly see it and be reminded of Hitler's power. It appeared on banners, posters, armbands, jewelry, and even dish towels. It was a sign that the Nazis were everywhere. After the war, several countries made it illegal to display a swastika.[11]

THE RISE OF THE "GERMAN CHRISTIANS"

There was at this time a group of pastors who stood solidly behind Hitler's rise to power. They carelessly tossed two thousand years of Christian beliefs overboard. They wanted a strong, unified German Church and a "Christianity" that was tough and aggressive, that would stand up and defeat their enemies. They boldly called themselves the **German Christians**. The German Christians wanted an official German church built upon Nazi ideals.

In these first chaotic days of April 1933, the German Christians held a meeting in Berlin. It was a disturbing event for anyone wary of Hitler's desire to make over German society. The lines between church and state were disappearing. The crowd was first told that they should expect their Führer to *führ* (lead) them in every aspect of German life, including the church. It was just what Bonhoeffer had warned against in his radio speech.

The goal of the German Christians was to define being "German" as the exact opposite of being "Jewish." In their eyes making Christianity "German" meant hacking away everything about Christianity that was Jewish. It was, of course, a ridiculous project, because Christianity is based upon **Judaism** (the beliefs and practices of the Jews). For starters, they decided the Old Testament must go. As the story of God and his chosen people, the Jews, it was obviously too Jewish. One pastor even went so far as to say that baptism and Communion were symbols of "German soil" and "the earth" instead of the body and blood of Christ.

Somehow, they forgot all about the Jesus who said "blessed are the peacemakers" and was humble, kind, and loving. One German writer described the ideal "love" of the German Christians. It had a "hard, warrior-like face. It hates everything soft and weak." Everything "rotten" and "indecent" must be "cleared out of the way and destroyed."[12]

After four hundred years of taking for granted that all Germans were Christians, no one seemed to know what Christianity was anymore.

THINK ABOUT IT

1. What was so dangerous about having a Führer? Why did the German people want one?
2. While Sabine and Gerhard were shunned by many, a few brave people declared that they were on their side. How important are kind words when you are at your lowest?
3. It's been said, "If you tell a lie big enough and keep repeating it, people will eventually come to believe it." Why does this kind of propaganda work?
4. Why was it so ridiculous that Jesus would be used in an anti-Jewish campaign?
5. What do you think about the German Christians' idea of "love"? How would this allow the Nazis to later do such terrible things?

CHAPTER 7

WORSHIPING GOD . . . OR HITLER?

1933–1934

If you board the wrong train it is no use running along the corridor in the opposite direction.

—DIETRICH BONHOEFFER

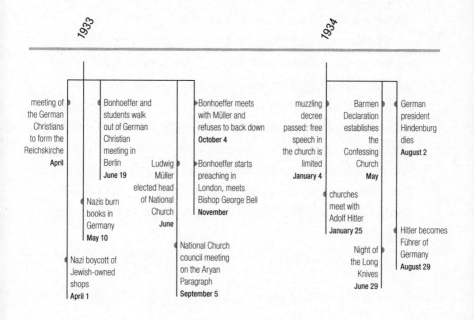

1933

1934

meeting of the German Christians to form the Reichskirche
April

Bonhoeffer and students walk out of German Christian meeting in Berlin
June 19

Ludwig Müller elected head of National Church
June

Nazis burn books in Germany
May 10

Nazi boycott of Jewish-owned shops
April 1

Bonhoeffer meets with Müller and refuses to back down
October 4

Bonhoeffer starts preaching in London, meets Bishop George Bell
November

National Church council meeting on the Aryan Paragraph
September 5

muzzling decree passed: free speech in the church is limited
January 4

churches meet with Adolf Hitler
January 25

Barmen Declaration establishes the Confessing Church
May

Night of the Long Knives
June 29

German president Hindenburg dies
August 2

Hitler becomes Führer of Germany
August 29

73

At first the newly formed German Christians were careful about hiding their most extreme beliefs from the German people. To most people, their meeting in April 1933 was the model of a calm, serious, theological gathering. But the German Christians made it clear that they wanted all German churches to be brought together as one church, ruled by the government. It was to be a **Reichskirche**, or a church of the "Reich." As a result of that calm April meeting, many Germans—who did not know the radical plans of the group—were open to a single Reichskirche, a government-run national church.

At the same time, one of Dietrich's closest friends, Franz Hildebrandt, was still determined to become a pastor. He had Jewish blood in him, so the Nazis were trying to force him out of the church and forbid him from preaching. Amazingly, on June 18, in the middle of the turmoil, Franz Hildebrandt was ordained as a pastor. But because he was a Jew, his future in the church could not have been more uncertain.

The German Christians held a meeting at Berlin University on June 19. Bonhoeffer and many of his students went to the meeting, but Bonhoeffer didn't make any comments. He let his students do that. Bonhoeffer had a bigger plan than just arguing. He and his students were all going to walk out if the German Christians proposed electing Hitler's man, **Ludwig Müller**, as bishop, or head of the national church. They did. At that point Bonhoeffer and his group stood up and made for the exits. To Bonhoeffer's surprise, 90 percent of the people in the meeting walked out too.

THE CHURCH ELECTIONS

Meanwhile, Hitler was moving ahead with his own plans for the church. He knew quite well how to deal with these Protestant pastors. "You can do anything you want with them," he once remarked. "They will submit . . . they are insignificant little people, submissive as dogs, and they sweat with embarrassment when you talk to them."[1] Then Hitler suddenly announced new church elections to be held July 23, to "choose" a leader of the church. This made it seem as if the people had a choice about who would lead the church. But with the Nazis in power, there was little question who would win.

Despite the stacked odds, Bonhoeffer and his students threw themselves into finding a candidate who could beat Hitler's man, Müller, but it was no use. When the church elections were held, it was a landslide; the German Christians received about 70 percent of the votes. Ludwig Müller was elected head of the German Christian church.

THE PASTORS' EMERGENCY LEAGUE

Soon after the election of Müller, Bonhoeffer received an invitation to become the pastor of a German-speaking congregation in London. He decided to accept the offer, but not before taking another swing in the fight against the German Christians. Before leaving, he passed out a paper he had written. He wanted to speak out against a new church law accepting something called the **Aryan Paragraph** that was coming up for vote soon. If passed, that law would keep people of Jewish descent out of the German church, just as they had been excluded from the government. Bonhoeffer suggested that German pastors could not reasonably serve a church that did not allow pastors of Jewish descent. The German Christians were not happy with him. It was decided that unless Bonhoeffer changed his opinion about the Aryan Paragraph, they would not send Bonhoeffer to London to represent the German church.

A national church council meeting was held in Berlin on September 5. Most of those who attended were German Christians, and 80 percent of the people wore the brown shirts of the Nazi uniform. It was less like a church council meeting than a Nazi rally. The Aryan Paragraph—the law against Jewish pastors in the church—was officially adopted.

For Bonhoeffer and his friend Hildebrandt, the time had come to split from the church. A church council had just officially voted to reject a group of people from Christian ministry simply because of their family or ancestors. And Hildebrandt, because of his Jewish ancestors, was one of them. Bonhoeffer and Hildebrandt called for the other pastors to take a stand against it. They asked them to quit their jobs in protest. But Bonhoeffer and Hildebrandt were like voices crying in the wilderness. No one else was willing to go that far just yet.

On September 7, two days after the Berlin church council meeting, Bonhoeffer and Hildebrandt made their outrage public. They wrote up an official protest and asked German pastors to sign it. It had four main points:

1. Everyone who signed it would declare their loyalty to the true Bible and to the beliefs of the church *before* the Nazis had come.

2. They would work to protect the church's loyalty to the Bible.

3. They would help by giving money to those being hurt by the new laws or by any kind of violence.

4. They would firmly reject the Aryan Paragraph—which said people of Jewish descent couldn't serve as pastors.

The written protest was sent to pastors across Germany. Much to the surprise of Bonhoeffer, Hildebrandt, and all involved, their statement of protest became very popular. The pastors across Germany who had signed this statement became an official organization: the Pastors' Emergency League. By the end of the year, six thousand pastors had become members. It was a major first step toward building a new church—a church that would later become known as the **Confessing Church**.

THE GERMAN CHRISTIANS GO TOO FAR

It was an electrifying time for the Nazis. The German Christians decided to celebrate the election of their new bishop, Müller, by throwing a massive rally. They did it in their favorite arena, the Berlin *Sportpalast*, or "Sports Palace," which had been used for cycling races, hockey, and ice skating events. The great hall was festooned with Nazi flags and banners declaring "One Reich. One People. One Church." Twenty thousand people gathered to hear the leader of the Berlin German Christians. This was his moment in the sun, and he seized it. But the speaker didn't know that his speech would be heard beyond the devoted German Christian audience in the *Sportpalast* that day. He eagerly spoke of the thoughts and plans of the German Christian movement. They were things that the German Christians had been saying among themselves all along—but they had never before said them in public. The sensible, reasonable mask they had been wearing in front of most Germans was now coming off.

In coarse, crude language, the speaker demanded that the German church must once and for all strip itself of every hint of Jewishness. The Old Testament would be first to go, with all its stories of Jewish history and heroes. Applause echoed throughout the stadium at his words. The New Testament must be redone, too, he declared. It must present a Jesus who fit the needs of the Nazi party. And it must no longer put too much "emphasis on the crucified Christ." Jesus' death on the cross was just too depressing and too much like a defeat. Germany needed hope and victory! They should also get rid of the apostle Paul and even the symbol of the cross, which the speaker called "a ridiculous" reminder of the Jewish people. Then the speaker went on to demand that every German pastor take an oath of personal loyalty to Hitler! And every German church must remove every church member of Jewish descent!

fanatic

(fə- 'na-tik) : a person with an extreme and uncritical enthusiasm or zeal, as in religion or politics.[2]

The speaker gave the performance of his life, but it was a fatal slip-up for the German Christians. In the morning the press reported that most Germans outside the packed *Sportpalast* meeting were outraged.

From that moment on, the German Christian movement

was largely doomed. The majority of German Protestants saw the German Christians as over-the-top, openly anti-Christian, and fanatically Nazi. Most of the Nazis, who were not Christians at all, simply thought the German Christians were fools.

THE LONDON CHURCH

In October, Bonhoeffer turned his attention to London. His job there was supposed to begin in two weeks. But he had been told that he must stop his protests against the German Christians or he might not be allowed to go to London as planned. Despite the threat, Bonhoeffer declared that he would never take back anything he had said or written. He even went so far as to demand a meeting with the Nazi bishop Müller himself.

Bonhoeffer met with Müller on October 4. When Müller asked him to remove his signature from the Pastors' Emergency League protest, Dietrich answered that he would not. Then Dietrich launched into a long quote from the confession of faith from his church—in Latin. Müller, who was not nearly as well educated, grew uncomfortable and cut him off. In the end, Müller believed that Bonhoeffer would cause him less trouble if he were in London rather than Germany, so Müller let him go.

While in London, Bonhoeffer still managed to keep closely involved in Germany's church struggle. He traveled to Berlin every few weeks. When he wasn't visiting Berlin, he was on the phone with someone there. His mother was as neck-deep in the church struggle as anyone. She fed her son every tidbit of information she could find.

If Müller had thought letting Bonhoeffer go to London might calm Bonhoeffer down or keep him at arm's length from

Berlin, he was dead wrong. In London, Bonhoeffer was five times the trouble for the German Christians than he ever could have been back home. London gave Bonhoeffer a freedom he didn't have in Berlin, and he used it well. He deepened his friendships and connections in the church world. And he made sure that whenever a positive image of Hitler's Germany showed up in the English press, it was quickly corrected with the true and shameful facts.

THE CHURCH BATTLE HEATS UP

After the German Christians' disaster of a meeting at the Berlin *Sportpalast*, the people shouted for Nazi bishop Müller's resignation. He was scheduled to be confirmed all the same. Even so, the German Christians were in an awful position and losing ground by the hour. So Müller passed into law something called the **muzzling decree.** Just as someone might put a muzzle on a dog's mouth to keep it from barking, he wanted to shut his opponents up. This law declared that discussions about the church struggle could not take place inside church buildings. Nor could they take place in church newspapers. Anyone who did so would be removed from the church. He went on to announce that all German church youth groups, called the Evangelical Youth, were to become part of the Hitler Youth.

THE HITLER YOUTH

Hitler wanted the absolute loyalty of every citizen in Germany—even the children. The Hitler Youth (or *Hitlerjugend* in German) was

---

IgorGolovniov/Shutterstock.com

**Hitler with Baldur von Schirach, who
was the leader of the Hitler Youth**

organized to teach children the ideals of Hitler and the Nazis. Boys were trained as future soldiers, while girls were trained to be ideal mothers and wives. Everyone was taught to worship Hitler, to hate his enemies, and to be good Nazis. Children were even encouraged to spy on adults and report to the secret police anyone who went against the Nazis' ways.

At age ten, a boy would be investigated to see if he was "Aryan" enough to join. If he passed the inspection, he would be admitted to the young people's division of the Hitler Youth. He would wear a uniform and be trained in things like marching, sports, shooting, fighting, and map reading. At age thirteen, he would be promoted to the real Hitler Youth, and at eighteen, he would become a full-fledged member of the Nazi party.

The girls would join the younger division at age ten. They would be promoted to the League of German Girls at age fourteen. Their lessons would be about "comradeship, domestic duties, and motherhood."[3]

Though the Hitler Youth may have looked like a summer camp from the outside, it was not about fun and games. Hitler said,

> In my [Hitler Youth], a youth will grow up before which the world will shrink back. A violently active, dominating, intrepid, brutal youth—that is what I am after. Youth must be all those things. It must be indifferent to pain. There must be no weakness or tenderness in it. . . . I will have no intellectual training. Knowledge is ruin to my young men. But one thing they must learn . . . to overcome fear of death, under the severest tests.[4]

Hitler was building a ruthless army. All young Germans were required to join the Hitler Youth. And if they didn't, their parents could be arrested.

Müller's decree was like a declaration of war. But Bonhoeffer knew that congregations like his in England had an advantage: they could threaten to break away from the German Christian church. They had power that the churches inside Germany did not. So the German pastors in England sent a telegram to the German Christians: "For the sake of the Gospel and our conscience we [join] ourselves with [the] Emergency League proclamation and withdraw our confidence from [Bishop]

Müller."[5] The next day, the Pastors' Emergency League within Germany planned to kick off its protest with a service at the magnificent and hugely important Berlin Cathedral.

Müller caught wind of their plans and decided to head them off at the pass. He got a police order to keep the massive doors of the cathedral shut. But even Müller could not keep the angry faithful from gathering in the vast plaza outside the cathedral, which they did. There they sang Martin Luther's famous hymn, "A Mighty Fortress Is Our God." The gloves had come off.

When the protestors sang outside the Berlin Cathedral, the song had a special meaning. "A Mighty Fortress Is Our God" was written by Martin Luther, a German who had long ago protested against the Catholic church and had started a new church that he believed was closer to what God intended. These Germans were doing the same thing. The lyrics of the song speak of a battle between good and evil, using the words of war:

A mighty fortress is our God [a fortress is a strong building that
    protects an army or a city],
A bulwark never failing [a bulwark is a wall built for defense]
Our helper he, amid the flood;
Of mortal ills prevailing ["mortal ills" are deadly troubles].
For still our ancient foe [a foe is an enemy—the Devil, or in
    this case Hitler]
Doth seek to work us woe [woe is misery];
His craft and power are great;
And, armed with cruel hate,
On earth is not his equal [the Enemy is powerful, and his
    weapon is hate].

> *And though this world, with devils filled,*
> *Should threaten to undo us;*
> *We will not fear, for God hath willed*
> *His truth to triumph through us [God uses us to fight evil, with*
> *his truth].*
> *The Prince of Darkness grim,*
> *We tremble not for him;*
> *His rage we can endure,*
> *For lo! his doom is sure,*
> *One little word shall fell him [God's power and truth will win in*
> *the end].*

A MEETING WITH HITLER

Eventually a temporary peace was agreed on. The overseas pastors put a hold on their threat to break away. And on January 17, both sides planned to meet with the chancellor, Adolf Hitler. In early 1934, many protesting church members still thought of Hitler as the reasonable one in all this, the man who would settle things in their favor. They were sure the smaller-minded men below him were to blame. It was Bishop Müller who was turning the church into just another Nazi organization, not Hitler—and when they could finally meet with the chancellor, all would be fixed.

But Hitler postponed the meeting. Then he postponed it again. Finally, on January 25, 1944, both sides met with Adolf Hitler. It did not go well for those who were opposing the German Christians. "I was very frightened," one representative said later. "I thought, what do I answer to all his complaints and accusations? [Hitler] was still speaking, speaking, speaking. I thought, dear God, let him stop." To try to put a better face on things, the representative declared, "But we are all enthusiastic about the Third Reich." Hitler exploded. "I'm the one who built the Third Reich!" he fumed. "You just worry about your sermons!" In that painful and sobering moment, the fantasy that the Third Reich was a reasonable movement was forever dashed. The only values of the Third Reich were the desires and will of a ranting madman—Adolf Hitler.[6]

Back in London, Bonhoeffer preached twice on his birthday, February 4, as he did every Sunday. In the evening he gathered with a few friends and got a phone call from his parents' home, where the whole family had gathered just to wish him a happy birthday. One of the letters he had received that day was from his father, who revealed something he had never said to his son before:

> Dear Dietrich,
>
> At the time when you decided to study theology, I sometimes thought to myself that a quiet, uneventful pastor's life . . . would really almost be a pity for you. So far as uneventfulness is concerned, I was greatly mistaken. That such a crisis should still be possible in the [church] field seemed to me, with my scientific background, to be out of the question. But in this as in many other things, it appears that we older folks have had quite wrong ideas. . . . In any case, you gain one thing from your calling—and in this it resembles mine—living relationships to human beings . . . in more important

matters than medical ones. And of this nothing can be taken away from you, even when the [situations] in which you are placed are not always as you would wish.[7]

THE CONFESSING CHURCH IS BORN

Bonhoeffer's superiors in the church were sick of the trouble he was causing them. He was summoned to Berlin for a meeting. His superiors did not waste words: Bonhoeffer must immediately stop reaching out to the other churches in London. Bonhoeffer refused.

While in Berlin, Dietrich met with other leaders in the Pastors' Emergency League. Their moment of truth had arrived. They agreed this was the critical battle that Bonhoeffer had been saying it was all along. They would hold a council to establish a new church at the end of May. It would be a turning point—an event that would officially and publicly separate them from the Reichskirche, the German Christian church. Bonhoeffer and the others had come right up to the line of no return, and they were readying themselves for the crossing.

Finally, in May 1934, the leaders of the Pastors' Emergency League held their first church council meeting in a town called Barmen in northwest Germany. It was there that they wrote the famous **Barmen Declaration**. Its purpose was to state what the German church had always believed. They wanted a new church that was grounded in the teachings of the Bible and set apart from the corrupt theology that had been coming from the German Christians.

On June 4—thanks to Bonhoeffer and his friend from

London, Bishop George Bell—the full text of the Barmen Declaration was published in the London *Times*. It dropped like a bomb, announcing to the world that a group of Christians in Germany had officially and publicly declared their independence from the Nazified Reichskirche. When one read it, it was easy to understand why they had done so.

The Barmen Declaration gave birth to what came to be known as the **Confessing Church**. The term *confess* means "to give agreement to" or "to acknowledge." It echoes Jesus' statement that "whoever confesses Me before men, him I will also confess before My Father who is in heaven" (Matthew 10:32 NKJV). The Confessing Church wanted to "confess" the real Jesus in the face of the false German church. Bonhoeffer wrote,

> There is not the claim or even the wish to be a Free Church beside the *Reichskirche*, but there is the claim to be the only theologically and legally legitimate evangelical church in Germany.[8]

CONFESSION OF FAITH

The Confessing Church treasured their right to "confess" their true faith—to say out loud what they believed. A confession of faith usually starts with "I believe" or "We believe." Chances are, you've heard a confession of faith before in your church. The next time you hear this familiar confession of faith in church, remember that you are blessed to have the right to say it out loud, without being arrested!

THE NIGHT OF THE LONG KNIVES

During that summer of 1934, dramatic changes were taking place in Germany. Aside from the chancellor, Adolf Hitler, the German government had another high office: the president. But ever since the democracy had been established after World War I, the office of president had been a weak one. The current president, Paul von Hindenburg, had made himself far less powerful than the chancellor, and Hitler had taken full advantage of that fact. Now eighty-six years old and close to death, President Hindenburg was a living, breathing link with Germany's glorious past under the kaiser. People still respected him.

coup d'état

(küd-ā-tä) : from French *coup d'état,* literally, "stroke of state (the government)," from *coup* "blow, stroke" and *de* "of" and *état* "state" : a sudden overthrowing of a government by a small group[9]

But then, President Hindenburg's doctors leaked the news that he was likely only months from death. Hitler feared that as soon as Hindenburg died, people would demand a return to the monarchy. He might be out of a job. Having sniffed the political winds with a nose of a bloodhound, he leaped ahead of the situation. And with wolflike ruthlessness, he ordered a savage bloodbath that came to be known as the Night of the Long Knives.

On June 29, an extraordinary murder spree was unleashed across Germany. Hundreds of people were slain in cold blood.

Some were dragged out of bed and shot; others were killed by firing squads. In later years, it was estimated that some four hundred or even as many as one thousand people were brutally murdered. When it was all over, Hitler claimed that the people his troops had killed had been plotting to overthrow the government. But with the help of God, he lied, it had been avoided. As usual, Hitler raged that he had been forced into his actions. He told the people that a *coup*—a mass betrayal—was in the works, that indeed his own life had been threatened. These murders, he declared, were in the best interests of the German people, for whom no sacrifice was too great!

On July 13, Hitler gave a speech:

> If anyone reproaches me and asks why I did not resort to the regular courts of justice [to punish the people], then all I can say is this: In this hour I was responsible for the fate of the German people, and thereby I became the supreme judge of the German people. . . . Everyone must know for all future time that if he raises his hand to strike the State, then certain death is his lot.[10]

It all had a chilling effect on most Germans. One of Bonhoeffer's students remembered the mood of the country that followed: "A crippling fear rose up like a bad odor within you."[11]

TRICKED INTO AN OATH

Three weeks later, President Hindenburg died at the age of eighty-six. Hitler was quick to announce his choice for Hindenburg's replacement—himself! He would remain chancellor as well. The two offices of president and chancellor would be combined into one person, because this was the will of the German people—at least according to Hitler. A vote was announced for later that month. Not surprisingly, ninety percent of the German people voted yes.

Playing on the deeply patriotic mood of the Germans mourning Hindenburg's death, Hitler called together the military officers and troops of the Berlin military base. By flickering torchlight, he asked them to renew their oath of loyalty. But when their hands were raised, they found themselves swearing an oath that was not what they had expected. It was not an oath to the German constitution or to the German nation, which would be normal for the military. Instead, it was an oath to the fellow with the mustache. According to what they were swearing, Hitler had become the living form of German will and law. The oath came to the point: "I swear by God this sacred oath, that I will [give] unconditional obedience to Adolf Hitler, the Führer of the German Reich and people, Supreme Commander of the Armed Forces, and will be ready as a brave soldier to risk my life at any time for this oath."

They pronounced these words all together, frozen in their lines and unable to even scratch their heads at what had just happened. They had been completely and magnificently tricked. Germans in general, and German military men in particular, took obedience and oaths very seriously. These few words, forced out of them, would pay off handsomely for the Führer in the years ahead. The German people found themselves far from shore, alone in a boat with a madman.

WHAT'S IN AN OATH?

Hitler tricked the German military members into making an oath to him. When you take an oath, the honorable thing to do—usually—is to follow it. You're supposed to do what you say you're going to do. But Jesus knew that oaths can be dangerous and used against you. It is best to be honest, but not make an oath. Jesus said:

> "Again, you have heard that it was said to the people long ago, 'Do not break your oath, but fulfill to the Lord the vows you have made.' But I tell you, do not swear an oath at all . . . All you need to say is simply 'Yes' or 'No'; anything beyond this comes from the evil one." (Matthew 5:33–34, 37 NIV)

THINK ABOUT IT

1. What did Bonhoeffer mean by saying, "If you board the wrong train it is no use running along the corridor in the opposite direction"? What should you do if you board the wrong train?
2. How was the Nazi church like a train going in the wrong direction?
3. Why did Hitler think that training young people in the Hitler Youth was so important?
4. What did Hitler think was "ruin" for his young people?
5. If Bonhoeffer were training youth to serve in God's army—an army of truth—what kinds of things do you think he would teach them?

CHAPTER 8

SECRET SEMINARIES

1934–1937

There is no way to peace along the way of safety. For peace must be
dared, it is itself the great venture and can never be safe.

—DIETRICH BONHOEFFER

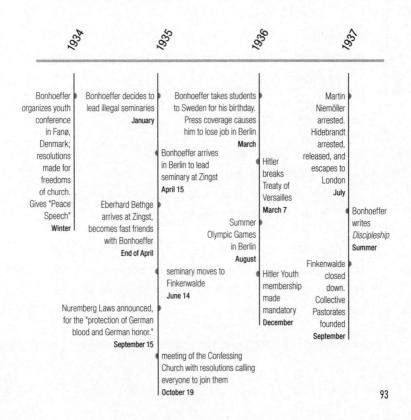

1934　1935　1936　1937

Bonhoeffer
organizes youth
conference
in Fanø,
Denmark;
resolutions
made for
freedoms
of church.
Gives "Peace
Speech"
Winter

Bonhoeffer decides to
lead illegal seminaries
January

Eberhard Bethge
arrives at Zingst,
becomes fast friends
with Bonhoeffer
End of April

Nuremberg Laws announced,
for the "protection of German
blood and German honor."
September 15

Bonhoeffer takes students
to Sweden for his birthday.
Press coverage causes
him to lose job in Berlin
March

Bonhoeffer arrives
in Berlin to lead
seminary at Zingst
April 15

Summer
Olympic Games
in Berlin
August

seminary moves to
Finkenwalde
June 14

meeting of the Confessing
Church with resolutions calling
everyone to join them
October 19

Hitler
breaks
Treaty of
Versailles
March 7

Hitler Youth
membership
made
mandatory
December

Martin
Niemöller
arrested.
Hidebrandt
arrested,
released, and
escapes to
London
July

Finkenwalde
closed
down.
Collective
Pastorates
founded
September

Bonhoeffer
writes
Discipleship
Summer

93

Bonhoeffer had been asked to give a speech at a Christian conference in Fanø, Denmark, that August of 1934. He also was asked to organize the youth conference that was part of the larger gathering. During the days of the conference, Bonhoeffer and the youth sometimes gathered on the Fanø beaches to discuss the events of the conference and the world as well as their own beliefs. During one seaside conversation, someone asked Bonhoeffer what he would do if war came. Bonhoeffer quietly scooped up a handful of sand and let it spill out between his fingers as he thought about the question and his answer. Then looking calmly at the young man, he replied, "I pray that God will give me the strength then not to take up a weapon."[1]

---

pacifism

(pa-sə-fi-zəm) : the belief that it is wrong to use war or violence to settle disputes

People become "pacifists" because:

- their religion speaks out against violence
- they believe that life is sacred
- they believe that war is a wasteful way to solve a problem when other solutions might be found

Bonheoffer wished "not to take up a weapon" because of his faith. But in Nazi Germany, being a "pacifist" meant you were not willing to fight for the Führer. That was a dangerous offense and could even be punished by death.[2]

There were people at the Fanø conference from all over the world, and they wanted to take action too. They wrote up a resolution—a statement of the freedoms they believed that Christians in the church should have. This resolution at Fanø united the voices of people from all around the world.

First, the resolution said that forcing people to take oaths and forbidding them from speaking freely was against "the true nature of the Christian Church." It asked for the following freedoms "in the name of the Gospel for its fellow Christians in the German Church":

1. "Freedom to preach the Gospel of our Lord Jesus Christ and to live according to His teaching"
2. "Freedom of the printed word and of Assembly [to write, speak, and gather freely] in the service of the Christian Community"
3. "Freedom for the Church to instruct its youth in the principles of Christianity," and freedom from being forced to accept teachings that went against "the Christian religion"[3]

Soon after, Bonhoeffer gave his famous "Peace Speech" to the crowd. "From the first moment," said one of his students from Berlin, "the assembly was breathless with tension. Many may have felt that they would never forget what they had just heard." The twenty-eight-year-old Bonhoeffer's words from that morning are still quoted:

There is no way to peace along the way of safety. For peace must be dared, it is itself the great venture and can never be safe. Peace is the opposite of security. . . . Peace means giving oneself completely to God's commandment, wanting no security. . . . [It is] laying the destiny of the nations in the hand of Almighty God, not trying to direct it for selfish purposes. Battles are won, not with weapons, but with God. They are won when the way leads to the cross.[4]

One student remembered that Bonhoeffer's last sentences were unforgettable: "What are we waiting for? The time is late." After Bonhoeffer finished, the leader of the conference came to the front and said that he didn't need to comment on the speech; its meaning had been clear to everyone.[5]

A DANGEROUS PEACE

Peace doesn't always mean the opposite of fighting. According to Bonhoeffer, it doesn't mean safety or security either. *Peace* means being right with God. In Bonhoeffer's case, being right with God meant standing up to Hitler, and even putting himself in a very dangerous situation. Here is what God's Word says about peace:

- Stop doing evil and do good. Look for peace and work for it. (Psalm 34:14 NCV)
- The LORD gives strength to his people; the LORD blesses his people with peace. (Psalm 29:11 NCV)
- Those who love your teachings will find true peace, and nothing will defeat them. (Psalm 119:165 NCV)

AN ILLEGAL SEMINARY

On October 19 the members of the Confessing Church met and issued a resolution of their own. They asked all "Christian congregations, their pastors and elders, to ignore any instructions received from the former Reichskirche [Nazi church] government and its authorities."[6] They asked Christians not to cooperate with anyone who continued "to obey that same church government." They called upon all Christians in Germany to join them. No one could say that the Confessing Church wasn't an official church anymore. Bonhoeffer was quite pleased, though he did hear through his brother-in-law Dohnanyi that Hitler had begun to turn his attention to the church struggle because of these very public troubles.

Earlier in the year, the leaders of the Confessing Church had realized that they must think about opening their own seminaries, or schools to train pastors. The Nazi-run church required that all university theological students prove their Aryan racial purity—they had to prove that they had no Jewish ancestors. Bonhoeffer's friends thought this was ridiculous and thought Bonhoeffer should run a Confessing Church seminary instead. But if he wanted to continue his work at the University of Berlin, he needed to decide soon. He was still officially a teacher there, but on a "leave of absence" to preach in Britain. And that leave of absence could not last forever. Finally Bonhoeffer made his decision. In mid-January, he wrote his eldest brother to tell him about choosing to lead an illegal Confessing Church seminary.

Dietrich preached his last sermons in London that spring. On April 15, he left for Berlin, ready to report for duty as the future head of the first seminary in the Confessing Church. Twenty-three pastors-in-training were ready, but there was still no place to house them. Then, on April 25, Bonhoeffer received word that the Rhineland Bible School building was free for the summer, and that it might fit their needs. The school was all the way on the northern coast of Germany, next to the Baltic Sea, in the town of Zingst.

At that time of the year, the beach at Zingst could be brutally cold and windy. But there were an old wooden farmhouse and a number of unheated, thatched-roof cottages on the grounds where the students could live. Everyone was young and up for an adventure, including Bonhoeffer. He hoped to conduct a sort of experiment in Christian living. Bonhoeffer had in mind a kind of community where the students would try to live the way Jesus commanded his followers to live in his Sermon on the Mount. The young men would live not just as students but as disciples of Christ.

BETHGE: A DEAR NEW FRIEND

One of the young pastors-in-training was named **Eberhard Bethge**. Bethge arrived on one of the last days of April, just after the evening meal. He immediately ran out to the beach, where everyone was playing soccer, as they often did at that part of the day. When Bonhoeffer realized that a new student had arrived, he left what he was doing. He greeted Bethge and invited him to take a walk along the beach. Neither young man could imagine how important their meeting would seem later.

The two men soon saw that they were more in tune with each other than anyone else in their lives. Each had extraordinary taste in literature, art, and music. They would soon become such close friends that many of the other students grew jealous. The pair had no inkling that their friendship would one day become the means by which Bonhoeffer's writings were preserved and spread throughout the world for generations.

A NEW HOME FOR THE SEMINARY: FINKENWALDE

The temporary and humble home of Bonhoeffer's school at Zingst had to be emptied by June 14. The Confessing Church seminary needed to find a more permanent home as soon as possible. They considered a number of properties, but finally settled on an old estate in Finkenwalde, a small town in what is now part of Poland.

The wealthy families in the surrounding countryside were strongly against Hitler and the Nazis. Most of them were devout Christians as well. Many families practically adopted the young pastors as their personal project. Wanting to help the brave, new seminary however they could, the community pitched in. One day the phone rang and the students learned that someone had sent Pastor Bonhoeffer a live pig. It was at the local freight yard, waiting to be picked up. Bonhoeffer himself donated his entire theological library for use by the students. He brought his gramophone and his many recordings, including his prized and exotic collection of negro spirituals from his days in New York.

Life in Finkenwalde had a daily routine. Each day began with a forty-five-minute church service before breakfast and ended with another service just before bed. One student remembered that the morning service began within minutes of waking up:

> Bonhoeffer requested us not to say a single word to each other before the service. The first word to come was supposed to be God's word. But this was not so simple, because we spent all the time in a room in which we slept six or eight at a time. . . .

We slept on old featherbeds, [on top of] hay mattresses. These mattresses had been used for generations. When you lay down on them, there was a huge dust explosion.[7]

The services took place not in the chapel, but around the large dinner table. They began by singing a psalm and a hymn chosen for that day. Then there was a reading from the Old Testament. Next they sang "a set verse from a hymn," using the same verse for several weeks, followed by a New Testament reading. They were supposed to meditate on the same verse for an entire week, for a half hour each day.

SPIRITUAL DISCIPLINES

Since the beginning of Christianity, believers have practiced "spiritual disciplines." These disciplines help believers to grow stronger in their faith and to know God better. Spiritual disciplines include:

- prayer
- fasting
- Bible study
- meditating on a Bible verse or passage
- living a simple life
- solitude, or spending time alone with God

- servicing others
- giving
- worshiping God
- confession of sins
- observing the Sabbath
- Communion (the Lord's Supper)

In which area would you most like to grow your spiritual muscles? How might you do that?

Bonhoeffer also took preaching seriously. For him a sermon was nothing less than the very word of God. It was a time when God would speak to his people. Bonhoeffer wanted to help his students see that preaching was not merely an exercise of the mind, as some thought. It was more like prayer or meditation on a Bible text. It was an opportunity to hear from heaven. For the preacher, it was a holy privilege to be the mouth through which God would speak.

MORE FRIGHTENING LAWS

On September 15, 1935, the **Nuremberg Laws** were announced. These were also called the "Laws for the Protection of German Blood and German Honor." They stated that "the purity of German blood is essential to the further existence of the German people." By that they meant that any bloodline, or family, that had a Jewish person anywhere in its history, was "impure." The laws said:

- "Marriages between Jews and citizens of German . . . blood are forbidden."
- Jews could not "employ female citizens of German . . . blood" as maids, housekeepers, or babysitters in their houses.
- Jews were "forbidden to display" the Nazi flag; they could only "display the Jewish colors," or flag. That was one of their only rights "protected by the State."[8]

The Nuremberg Laws began a second, "more ordered" phase of Jewish persecution. Jews, who were once legal citizens of Germany, were becoming subjects of the Third Reich. The

Nazis had drawn a line in the sand and everyone could see it. But Bonhoeffer believed it was the role of the church to speak out for those who could not speak.

AN ADVENTUROUS BIRTHDAY GIFT

On February 4, 1936, Bonhoeffer celebrated his thirtieth birthday. He had always felt overly conscious of his age and thought thirty was impossibly old. Oddly enough, it was the celebration of this birthday that would for the first time bring him into the sights of the Nazis.

It began innocently enough in one of the many conversations with his students in the main hall at Finkenwalde. They had been celebrating Bonhoeffer's birthday in the usual manner, with singing and other tributes. When the evening was winding down, they got into a rather rambling conversation about gift giving. Someone brightly suggested that the person celebrating a birthday should not receive the gifts, but rather should give them to his friends. When Bonhoeffer took the bait and asked what everyone might want, they settled on the idea of a trip to Sweden. Would he organize one for them? As it turned out, he would.

This was a grand opportunity for Bonhoeffer to show his students the church beyond Germany. He had entertained them many times with tales of his trips abroad. And he had explained that the church was something that went far beyond Germany's boundaries. It extended throughout time and space—to all places. There were many good reasons for such a trip besides just a new adventure. Bonhoeffer also knew strengthening his students' ties to churches abroad would help keep the Nazis from interfering with the seminary.

A SCANDALOUS TRIP TO SWEDEN

On March 1, the young pastors-in-training and their instructors boarded a ship and sailed northward to Sweden. They didn't know that the Nazis' German Christian church and the Nazi Foreign Ministry had already taken an interest in their adventure. Because Bonhoeffer had been so outspoken against the Nazis, they were already unhappy with him. And already, by 1935, making the Nazis unhappy was not a safe thing to do.

Bonhoeffer knew the dangers of such a trip. He had warned his students to be very careful about what they said, especially to newspaper reporters. The newspapers often took anything that was said against Hitler or the Nazis and made it sound even worse. So any word that Bonhoeffer or his students spoke against the Nazi government could cause problems for them. On March 3, the Swedish press put their visit on the front pages. The next day their visit to the head of the Swedish church made the papers too. Later, in Stockholm—the capital city of Sweden—they visited the German ambassador to Sweden. The ambassador, however, had just read a warning letter about this troublemaker named Bonhoeffer. So when Bonhoeffer and his students arrived, he greeted them coolly. At the time, Bonhoeffer didn't know why, but he later remembered seeing a life-sized portrait of Hitler in the room, scowling down at them.

With their arrival in Stockholm came many more articles and photographs. Each word of international press coverage made the German church look worse. The bishop fired off letters to the Swedish church and others, officially blasting Bonhoeffer:

[This trip] has brought Bonhoeffer very much into the public eye. Since he can be accused of being a pacifist and an enemy of the state it might well be advisable for the . . . church committee to [distance] itself from him and to take steps to ensure that he will no longer train German theologians.[9]

A corner had been turned. Bonhoeffer had been placed at the mercy of the Nazi state. Bethge wrote that "no form of [condemnation] was more fatal than the description 'a pacifist and an enemy of the state,' especially when this was used officially and in writing."

The immediate effect of the letters was that Bonhoeffer officially lost his right to teach at Berlin University. His long relationship with the world of universities and academics was over. But in some ways, for Bonhoeffer, the judgment was a badge of honor.

AN OLYMPIC-SIZED LIE

That summer of 1936 the Olympic Games were held in Germany, and athletes from around the world came to compete. The world did not yet know of the terrible things already happening in Hitler's government. The games gave Hitler a perfect opportunity to show the cheerful, reasonable face of the "new Germany." His henchman and minister of propaganda Joseph Goebbels spared no expense in building a masterpiece of propaganda—an enormous web of deceit, trickery, and fraud.

The Nazis did their best to show Germany as a Christian nation. The Nazis' German Christian church put up a huge tent near the Olympic stadium. Foreigners had no idea of the internal battle being waged between the German Christians and the

Confessing Church. It simply looked like there was a wealth of Christianity in the midst of Hitler's Germany.

In the meantime, Bonhoeffer continued his work with the Confessing Church. Most of their events and lectures were packed. Bonhoeffer warned the Confessing Church about getting too friendly with the Nazis—they had sometimes tried to speak reasonably about religious matters with Hitler and the Reichskirche. Bonhoeffer advised them:

> "Do not give dogs what is holy; and do not throw your pearls before swine, lest they trample them underfoot and turn to attack you" (Matt. 7:6 RSV). The promise of grace is not to be [wasted]; it needs to be protected from the godless. There are those who are not worthy of the sanctuary . . . grace has its limits. Grace may not be proclaimed to anyone who does not recognize or distinguish or desire it.[10]

Bonhoeffer did not want the Confessing Church to make the mistake of not taking a strong stand against the Nazis, or of giving them too much "grace."

OLYMPIC SPIRIT: JESSE OWENS

Hitler hoped the 1936 Olympics would be a showcase for Nazi ideals. He and Goebbels wanted to show off an Aryan "master race" that was better, stronger, and faster than the rest of the world. But American Jesse Owens was about to prove them wrong—on their own turf.

The Nazis didn't believe that the Jews were the only "inferior" people. They also believed anyone with African ancestors was non-Aryan, and therefore, inferior too. But then Jesse Owens came to Berlin. He was an African-American track-and-field star from Ohio. In the 1936 Olympics, he blew the competition out of the water, winning four gold medals for America. The Germans only won one in that event.

A special moment of Olympic spirit came during the long jump competition. The blond, blue-eyed German competitor, Luz Long, saw that Jesse was getting off to a bad start and gave him some advice: lay a towel on the ground and start a few inches before the jump line. Jesse took his advice and went on to win the competition. Though Luz Long had been beaten, he was the first to run up to Jesse after his jump, pat him on his back, and congratulate him on the field. The two men remained good friends until Luz died in World War II.

The German public loved Jesse Owens, even though an embarrassed Goebbels called Jesse's win a "disgrace." It was more proof that the Nazis were wrong—and that many German people, like Luz, didn't believe their lies. Jesse Owens held the Olympic record for most track-and-field gold medals for forty-eight years.[11]

THE NAZIS CRACK DOWN

Even when trampling personal rights and freedoms, the Nazis had been clever and careful up until this time. They were especially sensitive to public opinion. Their approach to the Confessing Church had been to try to squeeze it slowly out of existence. Churches were forbidden to read prayer lists from the pulpit. The passports of some church leaders were taken away so that they could not travel. In June the Nazis declared it illegal for the Confessing Church to collect offering money during its services. The avalanche of regulations and unjust laws over-whelmed the Confessing pastors, who were constantly messing up one of them and being arrested.

But in 1937, the Nazis stopped even pretending that they were being fair. They came down hard on the Confessing Church. That year more than eight hundred Confessing Church pastors and leaders were imprisoned or arrested. The outspoken **Martin Niemöller** was one such pastor. That June, he preached what would be his last sermon for many years. Crowds had over-flowed his church week after week. That final Sunday, Niemöller was no less honest than he had always been. He preached, "No more are we ready to keep silent at man's [request] when God commands us to speak. For it is, and must remain, the case that we must obey God rather than man."[12]

Bonhoeffer and his friend Bethge were in Berlin that day. The arrests of the Confessing Church pastors had been increas-ing, so they had planned to visit pastor Niemöller's house to come up with plan. But when they arrived, they found that were too late. The **Gestapo**—the Nazi secret police—had arrested Niemöller just moments earlier.

NAZI POLICE FORCES

Hitler and his Nazi officials needed thousands of men to carry out their ruthless orders on the streets of Germany. Much of the muscle they needed came from two police forces: the Gestapo and the SS.

The *Gestapo* was a dreaded group of men who acted as

criminal police, security police, and secret state police. They watched German citizens and hauled "undesirables"—or anyone who didn't fit Hitler's definition of a perfect German—off to prison or worse. The word *Gestapo* is a shortened version of the German words *Geheime Staatspolizei*, which means "Secret State Police." They were known for their sinister black cars and merciless roundups. They had the power to whisk people away for punishment at any moment.

The *SS* were "political soldiers" who worked with the Gestapo to run security and criminal police. They were trained to be hard-hearted killing machines. The SS were easy to spot in their slick black uniforms with the SS double lightning-bolt symbol. In 1939, there were over 250,000 SS soldiers. They were in charge of Hitler's safety, running the concentration camps, and later fighting in the army. *SS* is short for the German word *Schutzstaffel*, which means "protective troops."[13]

Bonhoeffer, Bethge, and Bonhoeffer's best friend Hildebrandt then met with Niemöller's wife to decide what to do next. As they were talking, several black cars pulled up to the house. Knowing these to be the Gestapo's secret police cars, Bonhoeffer, Bethge, and Hildebrandt made for the backdoor. But their escape was thwarted. They were stopped at the door by a Gestapo official. The three men were escorted back into the house, searched by another officer, and then placed under house arrest. They sat there for seven hours and watched as the Niemöllers' house was searched. The Gestapo searched until they discovered a safe behind a picture, full of money belonging to the Pastors' Emergency League.

Everyone but Niemöller—who had already been taken away—was released that afternoon. But things had definitely entered a new phase. Niemöller was in jail for eight months. Then on the day of his release, the Gestapo immediately arrested him again. They were known for just this kind of unpleasant trick. Hitler could not accept the freedom of someone so outspokenly against him. So he made Pastor Niemöller a "personal prisoner" of the Führer for the next seven years. Niemöller spent those years in a concentration camp. He would be freed by the Allies in 1945.

Bonhoeffer's friend Hildebrandt took over the preaching at Niemöller's church while Niemöller was in prison. His sermons were no less fiery than Niemöller's, and there were always Gestapo officers in the congregation. On July 18, ignoring the new laws, Hildebrandt read the prayer list aloud. He then took up an extra collection for the work of the Confessing Church. He asked that the money be placed on the Lord's Table at the altar, where it was dedicated to God and God's work with a prayer. The Gestapo usually turned a blind eye when churches broke these laws, but that day an officer boldly went forward and took the money.

After this, Hildebrandt was arrested. But instead of going quietly, he made a scene and then the whole congregation joined in! The crowd followed as the Gestapo officers escorted Hildebrandt to their car and watched as they tried and failed to start the car. After several minutes, the humiliated officers got out of the car and began walking with their prisoner toward headquarters. They were followed by the jeering crowd. Hildebrandt was taken from the Gestapo headquarters to prison.

Bonhoeffer and his other friends feared for Hildebrandt's life. He had Jewish ancestors, and even though he was a Christian, the Nazis still considered him a Jew. He was much more likely to be mistreated in prison. Thankfully, Bonhoeffer's brother-in-law Hans von Dohnanyi had been working undercover in the Nazi government, hoping to bring them down from within. When he saw what had happened to Hildebrandt, he stepped in and was able to get him out two days earlier than his sentence of twenty-eight days. Hildebrandt immediately fled to Switzerland, right under the authorities' noses. Without Dohnanyi's extraordinary help, Hildebrandt probably would not have survived. From Switzerland, Hildebrandt went to London where he immediately started to serve as a pastor at a church with one of his old friends. There, with the help of British supporters, he continued to work with other refugees. But Bonhoeffer would miss his friend.

THE COLLECTIVE PASTORATES

Throughout the summer of 1937, Bonhoeffer was overseeing a seminary course at Finkenwalde and finishing up a book on the Sermon on the Mount. The book had been taking shape in his thoughts since about 1932. The book, to be called *Discipleship*, would become one of the most influential Christian books of the twentieth century.

BONHOEFFER'S BOOKS: *THE COST OF DISCIPLESHIP*

Bonhoeffer's book *Discipleship* became one of the most famous books he ever wrote. Also known as *The Cost of Discipleship*, the book talks about what it means to be a disciple of Jesus, to accept his "costly grace" and to live like Jesus did. "Costly grace" means that being a disciple of Jesus comes at a cost—giving all of ourselves to Him. Great thoughts from this book include:

> "The world exercises dominion by force and Christ and Christians conquer by service."

> "Suffering [for Christ], then, is the badge of true discipleship. The disciple is not above his master. Following Christ means . . . suffering because we have to suffer."

> "A false faith is capable of terrible and monstrous things."

When the summer term was over, Bonhoeffer and Bethge took a holiday trip to the Bavarian Alps. After this they went up to visit Bonhoeffer's twin sister Sabine, her husband Gerhard, and their girls. It was there that Bonhoeffer received a surprise telephone call, telling him that the Gestapo had closed down the seminary at Finkenwalde. The doors had been sealed. An era had ended.

Bonhoeffer tried everything to reverse the closing of the seminary. But it was clear by the end of 1937 that Finkenwalde would not reopen. Still, Bonhoeffer knew this didn't have to mean the end of the illegal seminaries. They would continue in the form of what he called "collective pastorates."

First, he would have to find a church whose senior pastor was willing to help the Confessing Church. Then he would place a number of "apprentices" (his old students) with that pastor. In theory, they would be assisting the pastor. But in reality, they would receive the same education they would have received at Finkenwalde. These "collectives," or teams, of pastors were actually functioning as small seminaries, with one head pastor teaching the pastors-in-training.

The first collective pastorate was about a hundred miles northeast of Finkenwalde. The second was even more remote, about thirty miles farther east. In the second pastorate, Bethge would be the director of studies. This group of student pastors lived in what Bethge described as a "rambling, wind-battered parsonage . . . at the boundary of the church district."[14] Bonhoeffer split his time between the two pastorates, traveling back and forth on his motorcycle, weather permitting.

In 1939 the old parsonage house in Bethge's pastorate was no longer available, but even this was no hardship. The students relocated to an even more remote location. It was as if a bird were leading them farther and farther away from the cares of the present and into a realm deep in the heart of a German fairy tale.

THINK ABOUT IT

1. Why did Bonhoeffer think it was such a good idea to practice spiritual disciplines at his seminaries? How could those make his students better pastors?

2. "Bonhoeffer believed it was the role of the church to speak for those who could not speak." Who are some people who "cannot speak" for themselves today?

3. How can you and/or your church speak up for those people who can't speak for themselves? The poor? The homeless? The sick? The elderly?

4. Niemöller said, "No more are we ready to keep silent at man's [request] when God commands us to speak." Have you ever kept silent about something that you knew was wrong?

5. Why would Bonhoeffer have thought that losing his right to teach at Berlin University was a "badge of honor"?

CHAPTER 9

RUMBLINGS OF WAR

1937–1939

Christians in Germany will face the terrible alternative of either willing the defeat of their nation in order that Christian civilization may survive, or willing the victory of their nation and thereby destroying our civilization. I know which of these alternatives I must choose; but I cannot make that choice in security.

—DIETRICH BONHOEFFER, JULY 1939

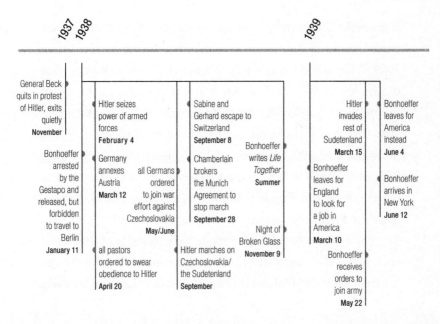

1937 1938 1939

General Beck quits in protest of Hitler, exits quietly
November

Bonhoeffer arrested by the Gestapo and released, but forbidden to travel to Berlin
January 11

Hitler seizes power of armed forces
February 4

Germany annexes Austria
March 12

all Germans ordered to join war effort against Czechoslovakia
May/June

all pastors ordered to swear obedience to Hitler
April 20

Sabine and Gerhard escape to Switzerland
September 8

Chamberlain brokers the Munich Agreement to stop march
September 28

Hitler marches on Czechoslovakia/ the Sudetenland
September

Bonhoeffer writes *Life Together*
Summer

Night of Broken Glass
November 9

Hitler invades rest of Sudetenland
March 15

Bonhoeffer leaves for England to look for a job in America
March 10

Bonhoeffer receives orders to join army
May 22

Bonhoeffer leaves for America instead
June 4

Bonhoeffer arrives in New York
June 12

The year 1938 was hugely chaotic for Germany and the rest of Europe. It was certainly so for the Bonhoeffers, and for Dietrich it did not begin well at all. On January 11 he was arrested at a Confessing Church meeting. Gestapo officers appeared, arrested all thirty attendees, and interrogated them at their headquarters for seven hours before letting them go. From that point on, Bonhoeffer was forbidden to travel to Berlin.

But, knowing many people in high places, Bonhoeffer was almost never without a solution. His father, Karl Bonhoeffer, used his influence in the situation. He was, after all, the most famous psychiatrist in Germany. He persuaded the Gestapo to make the ban only related to work: Dietrich wouldn't be allowed to preach or teach in Berlin. However, he could still travel there for personal and family matters.

"A STEW THAT THEY'LL CHOKE ON"

Bonhoeffer had many reasons to believe that Hitler's luck would soon run out. Hitler's troubles had begun on November 5, 1937. He called his generals to a meeting in which he spelled out his plans for war. For four hours Hitler laid out his plans to amaze the world with his military genius: "I'll cook them a stew that they'll choke on!"[1] He told the stunned generals that he would first attack Austria and Czechoslovakia to eliminate the possibility of being attacked on Germany's eastern side. But it was critical that England be soothed for the moment, he said, since the English were a serious military threat.

The generals left this meeting in various states of shock and fury. What they had just heard was pure madness. The foreign minister literally had several heart attacks. **General Ludwig**

Beck, who was highly respected and beloved by the German public, found it all "shattering." He determined that day to do whatever he could to stop Hitler's evil plans. From that meeting forward, the generals were focused on removing Hitler. Beck did all he could to influence the generals to stage a coup—a plan to bring Hitler down. Finally, to make as bold a public statement as possible, Beck resigned. But instead of telling the public all that Hitler was doing wrong, he exited quietly.

Hitler tightened his control by announcing on the morning of February 4—Bonhoeffer's thirty-second birthday—a drastic reordering of the whole German military. It was a bold, sweeping grab for power: "From now on I take over personally the command of the whole armed forces."[2] In a single stroke, Hitler abolished the War Ministry and created in its place the Armed Forces High Command, appointing himself as its leader.

INVADING AUSTRIA

Having successfully overtaken the German military, Hitler could once again focus on how to take over Europe. He started with his own birthplace, Austria. In March 1938, he boldly declared the annexation (*Anschluss*) of Austria. Just as an "annex" is the addition of a room built onto a house, Hitler meant to add the country of Austria on to Germany, making it part of his domain. For many Germans, this was a thrilling moment. Austria had once been under German control, but then had been taken away from Germany and made independent following the First World War. Thanks to their generous Führer, Austria would once again belong to Germany!

In the meantime, a new head of the Reichskirche, the

> Silence in the face of evil is itself evil. God will not hold us guiltless. Not to speak is to speak. Not to act is to act.
>
> —DIETRICH BONHOEFFER

Nazi-approved church, had been appointed, and he decided to give Hitler a tribute. On April 20 (Hitler's birthday), he published in the *Legal Gazette* a sweeping command that ordered every single pastor in Germany to take an oath of obedience to Adolf Hitler.

This decree brought bitter division to the Confessing Church at a time when things were already tense. Many pastors were tired of fighting, and they thought that taking the oath was a mere formality. It hardly seemed worth losing one's career over refusing to say a few words. Others took the oath, but with torn consciences, heartsick over what they were doing. Bonhoeffer and others saw the oath as a real threat and pushed the Confessing Church to stand against it. In the end, though, the church leaders did not stand up for what was right.

Then on May 28, Hitler informed his military commanders of his plans to march into Czechoslovakia and claim it for his own. In June, all fit Germans were ordered to join the war effort, and throughout the summer, Germany leaned toward war.

A DARING ESCAPE

The Leibholzes—Bonhoeffer's sister Sabine and her family—began to wonder whether their days in Germany would soon be over. Gerhard Leibholz's Jewish ancestry made them a target. A law was about to take effect requiring that a notice be put on every Jewish person's passport: if a person's given name was not obviously Jewish, Israel had to be added as a middle name for men, and Sarah added for women.

Hans von Dohnanyi, Bonhoeffer's other brother-in-law, urged the Leibholzes to leave while they still could. If war broke out, Germany's borders would be sealed. Sabine and Gerhard had heard stories of Jews being kidnapped at night. Every time the doorbell rang they were frightened, not knowing what trouble lay on the other side of the door. They had traveled to Switzerland and Italy on vacations and felt the freedom of being outside Germany. "Each time that we journeyed back [home]," Sabine recalled, "something like an iron band seemed to tighten round my heart."[3]

Finally it became too much: they prepared to leave Germany. It was a heart-wrenching decision. Sabine and Gerhard first went to Berlin where they discussed all the final details with the family, who had already begun to use code words in phone conversations and letters. They still hoped that with the plans to stop Hitler, they would be able to return home to Germany before very long. Perhaps they would only be away a few weeks.

SPEAKING IN CODE

Communicating in code was not only critical for the Leibholz's safety—it was common practice during the war. The United States used the Native American language of the Choctaw during World War I to keep their information from falling into enemy hands when it was sent over the radio or telegraph. The Germans were never able to crack their code. In World War II, the United States used the Navajo language as a basis for some of its military codes. Because the language is so complex, only native Navajos could use the code. These Native

Americans, known as Code Talkers, played a critical part in keeping American military plans safe.

Military Word	Navajo Word	Navajo Meaning
battleship	*lo-tso*	whale
fighter plane	*da-he-tih-hi*	humming bird
armor	*besh-ye-ha-da-di-teh*	iron protector
bomb	*a-ye-shi*	eggs
Navy	*tal-kah-silago*	sea soldier[4]

When Sabine and her family returned to their home on September 8, Bonhoeffer and his good friend Eberhard Bethge followed from Berlin in Bonhoeffer's car. The plan was to go with them for part of the journey to the Swiss border the following day. Everything was done in complete secrecy. Even the girls' nanny could not know.

The next day was a Friday. The nanny woke the girls at six thirty and began to get them ready for school. Suddenly their mother came into the room and announced that they were not going to school. They would be going on a trip to the beautiful vacation town of Wiesbaden! Eleven-year-old Marianne suspected something more was happening. They never went to Wiesbaden. But she was wise enough to know that if they were about to leave their home, she mustn't give away the secret. Sabine told the girls' nanny they would be back on Monday.

The Leibholzes' car was packed full, but not too full. They drove away in the two cars. When they felt it was safe, Sabine told the girls that they weren't going to Wiesbaden after all. They were going to cross the border into Switzerland.

Many years later Marianne recalled that day:

The roof of our car was open, the sky was deep blue, the countryside looked marvelous in the hot sunshine. I felt there was
complete solidarity between the four grown-ups. I knew that
unaccustomed things would be asked of us children from now
on but felt proud of now being allowed to share the real troubles
of the adults. I thought if I could do nothing against the Nazis
myself I must at the very least co-operate with the grown-ups
who could. Christiane and I spent most the time singing in the
car, folk songs and rather militant songs about freedom, my
mother, Uncle Dietrich and "Uncle" Bethge singing with us.[5]

When the Nazis demanded that every Jew in Germany have
a *J* stamped on his or her passport, it was clear that Bonhoeffer's
sister and her family could not return to Germany as long as
Hitler was in power. They would leave Switzerland for London.
There Bonhoeffer connected them with friends, who welcomed
them, as they had welcomed so many Jewish refugees from the
Third Reich. Gerhard eventually was able to get a teaching job
at Oxford.

NEVER TOO YOUNG TO HELP

Just because you are young doesn't mean you have no part in fighting
injustice. The Leibholz children played along with their parents in their
dangerous plan to escape. With the help of courageous adults today, you
too can join the cause of making the world a more just place. You can:

- do odd jobs to help support a child through a charity like World Vision (www.worldvision.org), fighting poverty and hunger
- join a group to volunteer at a local women's or homeless shelter, speaking out for those who can't speak out for themselves
- check with your parents, your school, or your church for ideas and organizations to help you do your part to make the world a better place

You can make a difference by giving your time and your prayers, by raising funds, or just by speaking out.

After seeing Sabine, Gerhard, and the girls off, Bonhoeffer and Bethge returned to the Leibholzes' house, where they stayed for several weeks. There Bonhoeffer wrote his small devotional classic, *Life Together*—a book about living in a Christian community.

BONHOEFFER'S BOOKS: *LIFE TOGETHER*

People cannot live life apart from community with other people. Even though being part of a community can sometimes be hard, it can also be where God shows up the most. Bonhoeffer's book *Life Together* talks about fellowship and loneliness, and how to live with and love others—even your enemies—as Christ would.

"Jesus Christ lived in the midst of his enemies. At the end all his disciples deserted him. On the cross he was utterly alone, surrounded by evildoers and mockers. For this cause he had come, to bring peace to the enemies of God. So the Christian, too, belongs not in the seclusion of a cloistered life but in the thick of foes. There is his commission, his work."[6]

CHAMBERLAIN'S CHEAP GRACE

While Bonhoeffer wrote *Life Together*, Hitler's attack on Czechoslovakia was front and center. Hitler publicly said that all the German-speaking people of Europe belonged to Germany. The Austrian annexation had been painted not as an act of war, but as a loving father welcoming his children home. The parts of Czechoslovakia that spoke German—or what was called the **Sudetenland**—were portrayed in the same way.

The army generals were aching for Hitler to march on the Sudetenland in Czechoslovakia, but not because they thought it wise. They thought that march would be so outrageous and foolish that it would give them the opportunity they had been waiting for: they would seize Hitler and take over the government.

As things stood that September, Hitler was on the verge of marching into Czechoslovakia. All the European leaders were expecting him to do it. It seemed unavoidable. They were preparing to stop him with their armed forces, and their plan would have worked. Germany was simply not ready for a war this big. The scene was set. But what played out on the world stage in the weeks ahead was stranger than fiction.

The breathtaking climax of this drama was destroyed by Britain's prime minister, **Neville Chamberlain**. The sixty-nine-year-old prime minister had never been in an airplane before, but he would now fly seven hours from London to Berchtesgaden on the far side of Germany to meet with Hitler, the ill-mannered tyrant. Chamberlain hoped to reach a peace deal. In what was eventually called the **Munich Agreement**, Chamberlain agreed that Britain and France wouldn't stop Hitler from invading Czechoslovakia (the Sudetenland), but only if Hitler would promise not to invade any other countries.

Chamberlain offered peace in exchange for a promise Hitler would never keep. Within a year, Hitler was marching across Poland, laughing at Chamberlain's weak deal.

KRISTALLNACHT: NIGHT OF BROKEN GLASS

In early November 1938, a seventeen-year-old German Jew shot and killed an official in the German Embassy in Paris. This shooting was just the excuse Hitler and the Nazi leaders needed to strike hard. In a "spur-of-the-moment" series of demonstrations, evils would be unleashed against the Jews of Germany on a terrible scale.

Hitler gave the command to take action against the Jews. An urgent message was sent to every Gestapo station across Germany. The orders gave specific directions on how to carry out the events of what has come to be known as the *Kristallnacht* (Night of Broken Glass). Jewish homes and businesses were destroyed and looted, synagogues were burned, and Jews were beaten and killed.

In his Bible that day or the next, Bonhoeffer was reading Psalm 74. What he read startled him, and with his pencil he put a vertical line in the margin to mark it, with an exclamation point next to the line. He also underlined the second half of verse 8: "They burn all God's houses in the land." Next to the verse he wrote the date: November 9, 1938. This was when Bonhoeffer most clearly saw the connection: to lift one's hand against the Jews was to lift one's hand against God himself. The Nazis were attacking God by attacking his people.

PSALM 74

Walk through the awful ruins of the city;
  see how the enemy has destroyed your sanctuary. . . .
They burned your sanctuary to the ground.
  They defiled the place that bears your name.
Then they thought, "Let's destroy everything!"
  So they burned down all the places where God was worshiped.
How long, O God, will you allow our enemies to insult you?
  Will you let them dishonor your name forever? . . .
Remember your covenant promises,
  for the land is full of darkness and violence!
Don't let the downtrodden be humiliated again.
  Instead, let the poor and needy praise your name.

—Psalm 74: 3, 7–8, 10, 20–21 NLT

A former student of Bonhoeffer's recalled what Dietrich was like during that time. When he saw what the Jews were going through after the Night of Broken Glass, Dietrich was "driven by a great inner restlessness, a holy anger. . . . During those ugly days we learned to understand—not just human revenge, but the prayer of the so-called psalms of vengeance which give over to

God alone the case of the innocent, 'for his name's sake.' . . . For him prayer was the display of the strongest possible activity."[7]

EVIDENCE FOR THE RESISTANCE

It's impossible to say when Bonhoeffer joined the conspiracy against Hitler. That's mainly because he was always in the midst of it, even before it could have been called a conspiracy. The Bonhoeffer family had relationships with many powerful people in the government, most of whom shared their anti-Hitler views.

Then there was Hans von Dohnanyi, Bonhoeffer's brother-in-law. He was a lawyer who was one of the conspiracy's leaders. In 1933, he was assigned to work with the Nazis' Minister of Justice and saw the inner workings of the Nazi leadership. But he cleverly avoided any connection to the party.

During 1938, Dohnanyi helped provide British intelligence with information about Hitler and the Nazis, trying to influence them into taking a tough stand against Hitler before he marched into Austria and the Sudetenland (Czechoslovakia).

The head of the German Military Intelligence was **Admiral Wilhelm Canaris.** His anti-Hitler views made him a perfect ally to the conspiracy. Canaris appointed Dohnanyi to his staff and asked him to compile a file of the Nazis' crimes and atrocities. Canaris knew that the evidence of these terrible evils would be crucial in convincing the generals and others to join the coup to overthrow Hitler when the time came.

Much of this information collected by Dohnanyi found its way to his brothers-in-law and their families. Before others in Germany knew of them, the Bonhoeffers heard of the mass murders in

Poland and the burning of synagogues there. Things that no one would know about for years were known in the Bonhoeffer household almost as quickly as they happened. Dohnanyi kept a file of these things. It was labeled "the **Chronicle of Shame**," but it later became known as the Zossen File, because it was eventually hidden—and found—in the town of Zossen, south of Berlin.

BACK TO AMERICA

On January 23, 1939, Bonhoeffer's mother told him that she had seen a notice ordering all men born in 1906 and 1907 to register with the military. Bonhoeffer would now be forced either to fight or to find a way out. There was one possible solution. Bonhoeffer might be able to have his military call-up postponed for a year. Perhaps in the meantime he might return to America and work with the church there. As he thought about the possibilities, he decided he must speak with one of his old professors from America, who happened to be teaching in England at the time. So on March 10, Bonhoeffer and his friend Bethge took a night train to the coast. The next day they made the Channel crossing into England.

On March 15, Hitler broke his agreement with British Prime Minister Chamberlain by marching into more of Czechoslovakia. To save face, Chamberlain vowed to declare war if Hitler marched on Poland. War was coming.

In England, Bonhoeffer met with his old professor. He explained that getting an official invitation to teach at Union Seminary in New York for a year would save him from being forced to fight for the Nazis. But it would be needed quickly. The professor leaped into action.

The next day, the Reichskirche (the Nazi church) published a new declaration. It stated that the Nazis were just carrying on "the work of Martin Luther" and that the Christian faith was the "religious opposite to Judaism."[8] It also accused other international church organizations of being corrupt. The Nazis were saying that being a Christian meant standing against the Jews, and that the Nazi church was the truest version of Christianity in the world. This, of course, was outrageously false.

The World Council of Churches wrote a response, rejecting the idea that race, national identity, or ethnic background had anything to do with actual Christian faith. It also declared, "The Gospel of Jesus Christ is the fulfillment of the Jewish hope. . . . The Christian church . . . rejoices in . . . community with those of the Jewish race who have accepted the Gospel." In other words, anyone was welcome to join the Christian church.

Bonhoeffer knew that he might be forced to join the military any day, but all he could do was wait and pray. Meanwhile, his old professor set Bonhoeffer's job search in motion. At last, on May 11, Bonhoeffer received a formal letter offering him a job as a pastor to German refugees in New York. He would also teach Union seminary courses. The job that had been created just for him should keep Bonhoeffer busy for "at least the next two or three years."[9]

On May 22, Bonhoeffer received a notice to report for military duty. He contacted the authorities, informing them of the job waiting for him in New York. On June 4, he was on his way to America.

On June 12, 1939, almost eight years since he had last left New York, Bonhoeffer entered the great harbor of America for the second time. But things were quite different now, for him and for the city. The New York skyline did not seem to grin at him as it did before. The building frenzy and the liveliness of the Jazz Age were gone. The **Great Depression**, which had taken its first steps back in 1929, was now ten years old, and like the rest of America, New York was sunk deep in poverty.

INVENTIONS OF THE GREAT DEPRESSION

You may have heard that "necessity is the mother of invention." That means if you have a need or an emergency, you're more motivated to try to fix it. The Great Depression was one big emergency. Millions of people were out of work and had to make the most of what they had. But those hard times gave us some great inventions:

- **The Supermarket (1930):** Michael Cullen was a manager at a small grocery store, and business was down. Nobody had money to spend. Then he had an idea: What if he opened a huge store that offered deep discounts to keep a steady stream of customers coming through the door? He quit his job and opened up the first supermarket—King Kullen Grocery—and it changed how we shop forever.
- **The Chocolate Chip Cookie (1933):** Ruth Wakefield was making a batch of chocolate cookies for the customers at her inn. She didn't have the meltable baker's chocolate the recipe called for, so she decided to "make do" with a chopped up chocolate bar. The Nestlé chocolate company eventually bought Ruth's recipe. They still print her Toll House Inn chocolate chip cookie recipe on the back of their packages.

- **Monopoly (1935):** The bestselling board game of all time was invented by Charles Darrow. He had lost his job as an engineer and was having trouble making ends meet. So he designed a game that gave people a chance to buy and sell real estate, spending huge amounts of play money when real money was hard to come by. It was a huge hit. Parker Brothers bought the game, and the rest is history.[10]

THINK ABOUT IT

1. What is a big injustice that you see in the world today? What steps can you take to right this wrong?
2. Bonhoeffer was "driven by a great inner restlessness, a holy anger" when he heard what was happening to the Jews. What makes you angry? Can anger sometimes be good?
3. Bonhoeffer did a lot to act against Hitler, but he thought prayer was "the strongest possible activity." Why would that be true?
4. Write out your own prayer for the things in this world that trouble you.
5. Look back at Psalm 74. Why did that verse remind Bonhoeffer of *Kristallnacht*—the Night of Broken Glass?

CHAPTER 10

THE GREAT DECISION

1939

At the end of the day I can only ask God to give a merciful judgment on today and all its decisions. It is now in his hand.

—DIETRICH BONHOEFFER

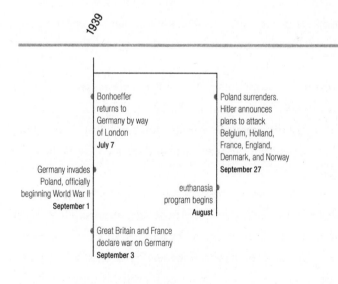

1939

Bonhoeffer returns to Germany by way of London
July 7

Germany invades Poland, officially beginning World War II
September 1

euthanasia program begins
August

Great Britain and France declare war on Germany
September 3

Poland surrenders. Hitler announces plans to attack Belgium, Holland, France, England, Denmark, and Norway
September 27

Bonhoeffer had not been in New York twenty-four hours, but he was already uneasy. His mind continued to churn about the situation back home. He was wondering how long he should stay in America, and whether he ought to have come at all. But he was always the master of his emotions; he didn't betray any of this anxiousness to his hosts. Only his diary gives us his thoughts:

> 13th June, 1939— . . . I do not understand why I am here, whether it was a sensible thing to do, whether the results will be worthwhile. In the evening, last of all, the readings and thoughts about work at home. I have now been almost two weeks without knowing what is going on there. It is hard to bear.[1]

> 15th June, 1939—Since yesterday evening I haven't been able to stop thinking of Germany. I would not have thought it possible that at my age, after so many years abroad, one could get so dreadfully homesick.[2]

Alone in his room, he wrote to his new boss, saying that he must go back "within a year at the latest."[3] Dietrich was obviously feeling guilty about leaving his job early. But then at long last he found peace in the Scriptures and decided it was the right thing to do.

On June 20, he was to have an important lunch meeting with **Henry Leiper**, who had given him the job in America. They met at the National Arts Club on Gramercy Park. Afterward he wrote in his diary: "The decision has been made. I have refused. They were clearly disappointed, and rather upset. It probably means more for me than I can see at the moment. God alone knows what."[4]

Years later, Leiper recalled their lunch meeting there, under the famous tiled ceiling of the exclusive club. He had looked forward to the lunch as much as Bonhoeffer had dreaded it; he expected to discuss the work they would do together. "What was my surprise and dismay," Leiper said, "to learn from my guest that he had just received an urgent appeal from his [coworkers] in Germany to return at once for important tasks [in the conspiracy against Hitler] which they felt he alone could perform."[5] Bonhoeffer was determined to obey God and was sure he was doing so in deciding to return to Germany.

He set his face toward Berlin. Somehow he was again at peace. He had been in New York only twenty-six days.

> *7th July, 1939*—Farewell half past eleven, sail at half past twelve. Manhattan by night; the moon over the skyscrapers. It is very hot. The visit is at an end. I am glad to have been over and glad that I am on the way home. Perhaps I have learnt more in this month than in a whole year nine years ago; at least I have acquired some important insight for all future decisions. Probably this visit will have a great effect on me. *In the middle of the Atlantic Ocean.*[6]

Bonhoeffer stopped in England for ten days to visit his beloved sister Sabine, Gerhard, and their daughters. When he arrived in Berlin on July 27, he immediately traveled to the remote town of Sigurdshof—where one of the collective pastorates was—to continue his work with the pastors-in-training there. While he had been gone, he discovered, **Hellmut Traub** had taken over where Bonhoeffer had left off. Traub recalled his surprise at seeing Bonhoeffer suddenly returned to them:

I was happy to know that Bonhoeffer was not in Germany, but safe from the coming reign of terror, and the catastrophe which I was convinced would follow. He must not perish in it. . . . apart from the great danger of his situation, Bonhoeffer was sure to find no mercy [from the Nazis], as he was bound to be a conscientious objector [and refuse to fight in the army]. There was no room for him in this present-day Germany. . . .

And then one day, after a short message that he was returning, Bonhoeffer stood before us. This was quite unexpected—indeed, there was always something extraordinary about him, even when the circumstances were quite ordinary. I was immediately up in arms, blurting out how could he come back after it had cost so much trouble to get him into safety—safety for us, for our cause; here everything was lost anyway. He very calmly . . . said that he had made a mistake in going to America. He did not himself understand now why he had done it. . . . He knew he had taken a clear step, though the [realities] before him were still quite unclear.[7]

He stayed and continued his work at Sigurdshof until that August. But there was a strong sense that war was coming soon. The village was so close to Poland, where the war would surely begin, that Bonhoeffer thought it too dangerous to stay there. He decided they must all leave. So the training ended early, and on August 26, Bonhoeffer was back in Berlin.

THE END OF GERMANY

Prime Minister Neville Chamberlain had vowed that Britain would defend Poland if Hitler attacked it. That time had come.

But Hitler couldn't simply attack. He had to make it look like self-defense. So on August 22, he told his generals, "I shall give a propagandist reason for starting the war; never mind whether it is plausible or not. The victor will not be asked afterward whether he told the truth."[8]

CRITICAL THINKING: PROPAGANDA TODAY

Hitler used propaganda to convince people to follow him. Believe it or not, people still use propaganda today—especially in advertising when someone is trying to sell something. How can you recognize propaganda? Here are a few things that stand out:

- **name-calling:** tearing something or someone down by using an insulting name, instead of using facts to support what is being said.
- **bandwagon:** the "everybody else is doing it" approach, hoping to make you feel left out if you don't join in.
- **testimonial:** paying a famous person to say something good about a product, hoping you'll believe and buy it, even though that person may not be an expert or may not even use the product.
- **the either-or lie:** giving only two choices, when more choices may actually exist. It is meant to make people choose sides by telling them, "If you're not for us, you're against us."[9]

The plan was for the SS to disguise themselves in Polish uniforms and attack a German radio station on the Polish border. To make the whole thing look more real, they would need German "casualties," or bodies of those Germans that the Polish were supposed to have killed. They decided to use bodies of concentration camp prisoners, dressing them as German soldiers. In the end, one man was murdered for this purpose. The deliberate murder of a human being in order to deceive the world seems a perfect opening act for what was to follow. This "attack" took place on schedule, on August 31.

In a reaction to the fake attack, German troops marched into Poland at dawn on September 1. The German **Luftwaffe**, or air force, rained bombs from the skies, deliberately killing civilians. The German armies on the ground also focused on killing civilians who couldn't defend themselves. It was a coldly deliberate act of terror never before seen in modern times. And it was Poland's first bitter taste of the Nazi cruelty they would come to know so well.

Hitler gave a speech afterward, casting himself in the role of victim. "You know the endless attempts I made for a peaceful . . . understanding of the problem of Austria," he said, "and later of the problem of the Sudetenland, Bohemia and Moravia. It was all in vain. . . . I am wrongly judged if my love of peace and patience are mistaken for weakness or even cowardice. . . . I have therefore resolved to speak to Poland in the same language that Poland for months past has used toward us."[10]

Admiral Canaris, the anti-Hitler head of the German Military Intelligence, had long dreaded this hour. He was overcome with emotion at the thought of what all this would mean. He told a fellow resistance worker, "This means the end of Germany."[11]

It now only remained for Britain to declare war. For two days the British tried to find a solution with diplomacy, but that Sunday, Great Britain declared war.

That morning Dietrich and Karl-Friedrich Bonhoeffer were

a few minutes from home, discussing the events of the last days. It was a warm, humid morning, with low-hanging clouds over the city. Suddenly there were sirens. World War II had begun. By war's end more than 80 of the 150 young men who had been Bonhoeffer's pastors-in-training would be killed.

In Berlin Dietrich met with his brother-in-law Dohnanyi, who told him everything, as he always had. But Bonhoeffer now heard things he had not heard before. Dohnanyi told him that now, under the dark cover of war, Hitler had unleashed horrors the world had never seen. Dohnanyi's primary source for information was his boss, Admiral Canaris.

Canaris and the others leaders in the German military thought that Hitler's savage nature was unfortunate, but they had no idea how bad it was. Since the SS committed the most wicked acts, Hitler could keep the worst of it from his military leaders. But reports leaked out. Many German generals were beside themselves with shock and fear.

Just as Hitler had been planning for years to enslave the Poles and kill the Jews, he had been planning to murder every German with a disability. Preparations for something they called the **T-4 euthanasia program** had been under way for years. *Euthanasia*, from the Greek word meaning "good death," is a word used to describe killing another person who is suffering, or allowing that person to die. But Hitler's euthanasia program went even further. In August 1939, every doctor and midwife in the country was notified that they must register all children born with genetic defects. They must also include all children born since 1936. In September, when the war began, so, too, began the killing of these "defectives." Over the next few years, five thousand small children were killed. It wasn't until later that fall that attention was formally focused on the other "incurables." These included the mentally and physically handicapped of all ages, as well as others who did not meet Hitler's perfect Aryan standards.

ETHICS AND EUTHANASIA

Bonhoeffer was clear about his feelings on euthanasia. Between 1940 and 1943, he wrote a book called *Ethics*. *Ethics* is the study of right and wrong behavior based on ideas about our moral responsibilities. The study of ethics helps us figure out the right thing to do. In his book, Bonhoeffer wrote:

"The idea of destroying the life of one who has lost social [use] comes from weakness, not from strength."

"Where, other than in God, should the measure for the ultimate worth of life lie?"

In the case of euthanasia, Bonhoeffer's answer was clear: God should decide who lives or dies, not the government.

On September 27, 1939, the day of Poland's surrender, Hitler gathered his generals and announced plans to make war on the western frontier too. He would attack Belgium and Holland. And then France and England. And Denmark and Norway.

Dohnanyi updated his Chronicle of Shame. He was able to collect actual film footage of many SS atrocities in Poland. They needed the proof. When everything was over, they didn't want the public to believe the lies that would certainly be told. A cover-up could not be allowed.

The things happening in 1939 were worse than anything Bonhoeffer had dreamed. But he couldn't even share what he knew with his best friends. It had become too dangerous. More than ever now, he was alone with God, and he looked to God's judgment upon his actions. This was when he began to realize that he was already part of the conspiracy to remove Hitler.

THINK ABOUT IT

1. Why did Bonhoeffer return to Germany from America?
2. Are you facing a big decision? Or is there an event coming that is worrying you? To help you figure out what to do, try following Bonhoeffer's example: journal about it. In your journal, try to:
   a. write honestly about your thoughts and opinions
   b. look for Scripture that applies to your situation
   c. list what's important to you
   d. write out a prayer
   e. remember events and conversations that help you think about your choice

CHAPTER 11

FROM PASTOR TO SPY

1940–1942

The German people will be burdened with a guilt the world will not forget in a hundred years.

—HENNING VON TRESCKOW

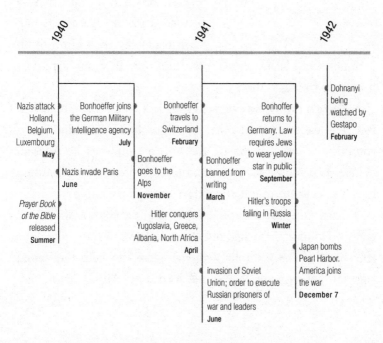

1940

1941

1942

Nazis attack Holland, Belgium, Luxembourg
May

Bonhoeffer joins the German Military Intelligence agency
July

Nazis invade Paris
June

Prayer Book of the Bible released
Summer

Bonhoeffer travels to Switzerland
February

Bonhoeffer goes to the Alps
November

Hitler conquers Yugoslavia, Greece, Albania, North Africa
April

invasion of Soviet Union; order to execute Russian prisoners of war and leaders
June

Bonhoffer returns to Germany. Law requires Jews to wear yellow star in public
September

Bonhoeffer banned from writing
March

Hitler's troops failing in Russia
Winter

Dohnanyi being watched by Gestapo
February

Japan bombs Pearl Harbor. America joins the war
December 7

Bonhoeffer was now at the heart of the conspiracy against Hitler and the Nazis. He gave emotional support and encouragement to those more directly involved, such as his brother Klaus and his brother-in-law Dohnanyi. Klaus Bonhoeffer was a lawyer who had connections in the Nazi government that he used to gain information. Hans von Dohnanyi was married to Dietrich's sister Christine. Dohnanyi was also a lawyer, but he had a position inside the German Supreme Court and was an agent of the German Military Intelligence—similar to a CIA secret agent. The Germans had no idea that he was working against Hitler, instead of for him. Both Dohnanvi and Klaus played important roles in supplying information to the resistance.

conspiracy

(kən-' spir-ə-sē):

1 : a secret plan made by two or more people to do something that is harmful or illegal; **2** : the act of secretly planning to do something that is harmful or illegal[1]

Dietrich didn't have personal worries about being involved. But as a leader in the Confessing Church, his situation was a complicated one. He wasn't free to do simply as he pleased. Whatever he chose to do, he had to consider others, including how his decisions might affect the Confessing Church.

Meanwhile, the conspiracy moved ahead with new life and energy. Dohnanyi reached out to the Vatican in Italy. The pope (the head of the Catholic Church) agreed to help the young German government that would form once Hitler was killed.

Britain would lend a hand too. It was all very promising. The conspirators planned a signal: when Hitler gave the green light to attack the West, they would work with the pope and Britain to overthrow him. It was decided that Hitler had to be killed, so an assassination was planned.

But how could a Christian pastor agree to help assassinate someone—even someone as evil as Hitler? Wasn't killing wrong? Dietrich's good friend Eberhard Bethge tried to explain:

> Bonhoeffer introduced us in 1935 to the problem of what we today call political resistance. The levels of confession [speaking out loud] and of resistance [taking action] could no longer be kept neatly apart. . . . We now realized that mere confession, no matter how courageous, inescapably meant [agreeing] with the murderers. . . .
>
> Thus we were approaching the borderline between confession and resistance; and if we did not cross this border, our confession was going to be no better than cooperation with the criminals. And so it became clear where the problem lay for the Confessing Church: we were resisting by way of confession, but we were not confessing by way of resistance.[2]

Talking about resistance was no longer enough. Bonhoeffer came to believe that doing nothing would be just as evil as helping the Nazis do their terrible deeds. So Bonhoeffer decided to do something. He decided to help the resistance get rid of Hitler. Bonhoeffer would get his hands dirty, not because he had grown impatient, but because God was telling him it was time to act.

THE POINT OF NO RETURN

Hitler ordered his armies to march westward in May of 1940. On the tenth of May, German units attacked Holland. The Dutch submitted to the Nazis within five days. Belgium was next, and soon German tanks were roaring across France. On June 14, German troops marched into Paris, and three days later, their cries of surrender were heard round the world.

Meanwhile, back in Germany, Bonhoeffer and his friend Bethge were visiting an old seminary friend. After a pastors' meeting that morning, they found an outdoor café in the sun. Suddenly a trumpet blast over the radio loudspeakers announced a special news flash: *France has surrendered!*

People went wild. Some of them leaped up and stood on chairs; others stood on tables. Everyone threw out his arm in the Nazi salute and burst into singing the national anthem. It was an explosion of patriotism, and Bonhoeffer and Bethge were pinned like beetles. They couldn't be caught not celebrating! It would give them away. Bonhoeffer stood up and threw out his arm in the "Heil, Hitler!" salute. As Bethge stood staring at his friend in shock, Bonhoeffer whispered to him: "Are you crazy? Raise your arm! We'll have to run risks for many different things, but this silly salute is not one of them!"[3]

Bethge realized that Bonhoeffer had crossed a line. He was playing the part because he was involved in the secret plot. He didn't want to be thought of as an objector. He wanted to blend in. He didn't want to make an anti-Hitler statement at that moment. He had bigger fish to fry. Bethge said that he knew at that café, when Bonhoeffer was saluting Hitler, that his friend had reached a point of no return. Bonhoeffer had crossed from "confession" to "resistance."

STILL A PASTOR AND WRITER

As his role in the conspiracy developed, Bonhoeffer continued his church work and his writings. The last book he published in his lifetime was *The Prayerbook of the Bible*, which appeared in 1940. It was a book on the Old Testament Psalms, written at a time when the Old Testament was considered "too Jewish" to be accepted by the Nazis. His willingness to release a book on such an unpopular theme proved his devotion to the truth of the Bible.

The Prayerbook of the Bible was a passionate statement of the importance of the Old Testament to Christianity and to the church. He claimed that Christianity and Christ were unavoidably Jewish, and that the Psalms were critically important in Jesus' prayers. The Old Testament was not just the foundation of the New Testament; it was also part of it. Bonhoeffer's book was a brave criticism of the Nazis' efforts to undermine anything Jewish.

THE POWER OF PSALMS

The word *psalm* actually means "song." Right in the middle of your Bible sits a book of 150 songs, all written to praise God. King David wrote some of them, while others were passed down through time and tradition. But these songs aren't just for singing; they are also for prayer. Jesus quoted from them many times. His last words—"My God, my God, why have you forsaken me?" (Matthew 27:46 NIV)— were even a quote from Psalm 22:1.

There's a prayer in the book of Psalms for every need. Here is
one that Bonhoeffer might have prayed when praising God:

Hear my prayer, Lord God Almighty;
    listen to me, God of Jacob. . . .
Better is one day in your courts
    than a thousand elsewhere;
I would rather be a doorkeeper in the house of my God
    than dwell in the tents of the wicked.
For the Lord God is a sun and shield;
    the Lord bestows favor and honor;
no good thing does he withhold
    from those whose walk is blameless.
Lord Almighty,
    blessed is the one who trusts in you!

Psalm 84:8, 10–12 NIV

SECRET AGENT BONHOEFFER

On July 14, 1940, Bonhoeffer was preaching at a church conference when the Gestapo arrived and broke up the meeting.
They announced a new order forbidding such meetings, and
the conference ended. No one was arrested, but Bonhoeffer saw
that his freedom to preach was coming to an end. Soon after,
Bonhoeffer returned to Berlin and spoke with Dohnanyi about
his plans going forward. He had to find somewhere else to focus
his talents.

There was a great rivalry between the German Military
Intelligence agency (where Dohnanyi worked) and the Gestapo.

But since they were separate agencies—just as the CIA and the FBI are in the United States—Dohnanyi thought that if the Military Intelligence officially employed Bonhoeffer, the Gestapo would be forced to leave him alone. It made sense for many reasons. As an agent, Bonhoeffer would have great freedom of movement to continue his work as a pastor. Even better, he would have the perfect cover to expand his work with the conspiracy against Hitler. Another benefit of being part of Military Intelligence was that Bonhoeffer was unlikely to be called to fight in the Nazi army.

Dohnanyi's boss in the Military Intelligence agency, Admiral Canaris, was anti-Hitler too. He was an honorable man, but said that the Nazi government was filled with "such sinister immorality that traditional values and loyalties no longer applied."[4] Because of that he had joined the conspiracy against Hitler. But for many in the Confessing Church, such trickery was no different from lying.

So Bonhoeffer was forced to choose. On the one hand, as a Military Intelligence agent, he would appear to be a Nazi supporter. After everything he had said against the Nazis, people were sure to be confused. On the other hand, he would be secretly working to bring down Hitler. Some might call that lying and killing. Bonhoeffer had moved into a very lonely place indeed. No one outside the conspiracy could know what he was up to.

Dohnanyi, Bethge, Bonhoeffer, and the other members of the resistance decided to move forward. The day had come. Bonhoeffer had officially joined the conspiracy. He would be shielded by the protection of the Nazi Military Intelligence agency. And in the disguise of a member of that agency, he would be protected by the resistance leaders working within it too.

There were several layers of deception. First, Bonhoeffer

would be still be preaching and continuing his theological writing, as he wished to do. Officially, he would tell the Nazis that being a pastor was a front, that he was a "secret agent" working in the church for the Nazis. But in reality, his work as an agent was a front for his real work—as a conspirator *against* the Nazis. It was a risky cat-and-mouse game to play with Hitler's henchmen.

> **subversive**
>
> (səb-vər-siv): secretly trying to ruin or destroy a government, political system, etc.[5]

Bonhoeffer's enemies still remembered his earlier words against the Nazis, and some officials tried to ban him from speaking in public. They said it was because of his "subversive activities." The resistance caught wind of this and had no choice but to step in and protect him.

TRAVEL UNDER COVER

Through his connections, Bonhoeffer was whisked away to a remote and scenic Catholic monastery, nestled in the Bavarian Alps. For Bonhoeffer, it was a small dream come true. Here, in this Catholic stronghold of resistance against the Nazis, he found deep peace and quiet, far from the mental noise of Berlin. Bonhoeffer became friendly with the priests there, who invited him to stay as their guest as long as he liked. Beginning in November, he lived there through the winter.

Later in February 1941, the resistance sent Bonhoeffer on an assignment in Geneva, Switzerland. His main purpose there was to make contact with Protestant leaders outside Germany.

He was to let them know about the conspiracy and to see if they would support a new government after the assassination and takeover. But at first, Bonhoeffer couldn't even get into Switzerland. The Swiss border police insisted that someone inside Switzerland must first vouch for him as a sponsor. Bonhoeffer named Karl Barth, his former teacher. Barth was from Switzerland, and one of the most famous theologians in the world. He had been a great role model to Dietrich, and Barth agreed to be responsible for him—though he still had some doubts about Dietrich.

Like others at the time, Barth was confused about Bonhoeffer's mission. How could a Confessing Church pastor come to Switzerland in the midst of war? Wasn't he running away from his job? It also seemed to him that Bonhoeffer must have somehow made peace with the Nazis.

Such doubts and questions from others would torment Bonhoeffer during this time. But how could he explain what he was doing to those outside his inner circle? It was a secret, and he couldn't tell anyone, no matter how much he wanted to. People wondered how he had escaped being a soldier like the rest of his generation. To others, it looked as if he were writing and traveling, meeting with this one and that one, going to movies and restaurants, and living a life of privilege and freedom. How could he do this while others were suffering and dying?

For those who knew that Bonhoeffer was working for the Military Intelligence, it was even harder to understand. Had he finally given in, this outspoken pastor who always was so unyielding? Was this the same man who had boldly stood up against the Nazi church and asked them to stand up too? Was he now a traitor to his own cause?

Even if Bonhoeffer could have explained that he was work-ing against Hitler, many in the Confessing Church would still have been confused, and others would have been outraged. For a pastor to be involved in a plot to assassinate the head of state during a time of war, when brothers and sons and fathers were giving their lives for their country, was unthinkable.

Bonhoeffer was in Switzerland a month. When he returned to Munich at the end of March, he discovered a letter from the Nazi government informing him that he was now banned from writing. The pro-Jewish content of his book on the Psalms had not gone unnoticed.

TROUBLE ON THE FRONT LINES

In April, the Nazis' victories were so stunning and so rapid that most generals had lost all hope of standing up to Hitler. Yugoslavia, Greece, and Albania had been conquered, and the Nazis had won in North Africa too. Hitler seemed unstoppable, so most of his generals floated along with the rising German tide. They could not be persuaded to lift a finger against him. But those in the resistance knew that persuading the top gener-als was the only hope of toppling Hitler from the inside. They were stuck.

Then came June 6, 1941, and one of Hitler's cruelest orders yet. The Nazi military was planning to invade the Soviet Union—what is now Russia. Hitler instructed the army to shoot and kill all captured Soviet military leaders. The generals were horrified. Murdering all the captured leaders was unthinkable. It went against all codes of military honor.

PRISONERS OF WAR: THE GENEVA CONVENTION

There are rules for war, just like anything else. A particular set of rules, the Geneva Convention, has to do with how prisoners of war (POWs) are treated. After World War I, representatives from many countries met in Geneva, Switzerland in 1929. They all signed an agreement to protect the human rights of people captured during war.

Prisoners of war must be:

- treated with respect
- allowed to tell their families about their capture
- clothed and fed
- given proper bathrooms, soap, and water
- given medical care if sick
- allowed to practice their religion
- paid for any work they do
- allowed to send and receive letters, cards, and care packages

Prisoners of war must be *protected* from:

- violence
- dangerous working conditions
- all forms of cruelty and corporal punishment
- threats and insults
- sentencing or punishment without the opportunity to defend themselves
- acts of revenge
- being sentenced or executed without a trial

Germany signed the 1929 Geneva Convention too. No wonder Hitler's generals were so outraged by the things he was ordering them to do![6]

Later that June, the march of the German armies toward Moscow began. Germany was at war with the Soviet Union. With the help of Dohnanyi and other connections, Bonhoeffer kept a number of pastors in the Confessing Church from having to fight in the German army. He hoped to keep them from danger—and also keep them working as pastors. Their churches needed them more than ever.

BONHOEFFER CARRIES ON

While Hitler continued to wage his war across Europe and the Soviet Union, Bonhoeffer continued pastoring through his letters. In August he wrote a letter that was sent around to the hundred or so former students. Two men from the group of students had been killed in the fighting, and many more had been forced to fight on the front lines. Upon their deaths, Dietrich wrote these words:

> They have gone before us on the path that we shall all have to take at some point. In a particularly gracious way, God reminds those of you who are out on the front to remain prepared. . . . To be sure, God shall call you, and us, only at the hour that God has chosen. Until that hour, which lies in God's hand alone, we shall all be protected even in greatest danger.[7]

Although not on the front lines himself, Bonhoeffer heard from many of the young men who were. He encouraged them by return mail and prayed for them. One of them wrote to tell him that the temperature was forty below zero: "For days at a stretch we cannot even wash our hands, but go from the dead bodies to a meal and from there back to the rifle. All one's energy has to be summoned up to fight against the danger of freezing, to be on the move even when one is dead tired."[8] The young man wondered whether they would ever be allowed to return home again, to resume their calm and quiet lives. A short time later, Bonhoeffer learned that he had been killed.

By the fall of 1941, Britain had dropped out of the plan to overthrow Hitler from within. The war had dragged on too long. With Germany fighting Russia, Winston Churchill, who was now Britain's prime minister, saw it as all or nothing. He was not interested in the German resistance's conspiracy—if one even existed.

As Germany's armies moved toward Moscow, the SS was free to unleash its cruelty on anyone who crossed its path. Thousands of innocent and defenseless people were killed in the most horrible ways. As a result of such things, many more in the army leadership were driven to join the conspiracy against Hitler. At one point, officers went up to one of their higher ranking field marshals and begged him with tears in their eyes to stop the executions going on in front of them. But despite his high rank, he was powerless to stop the SS. His demands that the SS commander in charge of the massacres be brought to him were met with defiant laughter. Hitler had given the SS free rein, and even a field marshal could do nothing about it.

When Bonhoeffer returned from Switzerland in late September, he learned of still more horrors. A new law required all Jews in Germany to wear a yellow star in public. At the Dohnanyis' house, Bonhoeffer famously said that, if needed, he would be willing to kill Hitler himself. First, however, he said he would have to resign from the Confessing Church.

HITLER STUMBLES

In October 1941, the German generals on the Russian front were becoming more and more annoyed with the Führer's tactics. Between this and the awful cruelty of the SS, many were finally ready to turn against him.

The tide was turning against Adolf Hitler. The rest of his eastern armies were now charging into the white jaws of the notorious Russian winter. The cold's fury increased with each day. Thousands of German soldiers were dying from severe frostbite. Fuel was freezing. Fires had to be lit under tanks in order to start them. Because of the cold, machine guns stopped firing.

Still, Hitler cruelly drove his armies forward. On December 4, the temperature fell to thirty-one degrees below zero. On the fifth, it fell to thirty-six below zero—cold enough to cause frostbite after just a few minutes of exposure. On the sixth of December, the Russians attacked the German lines with shattering force. The once invincible armies of Adolf Hitler turned tail and went into full retreat.

The reversal in the Soviet Union pierced Hitler like a dagger. But the news on December 7 of the sneaky Japanese attack on Pearl Harbor revived his spirits. The Japanese had attacked the American base in Hawaii with hundreds of fighter planes. More than two thousand American soldiers and sailors had died, and America was now in the war. Hitler especially rejoiced at the underhandedness of the attack. No one had seen it coming, and Hitler said that was much like his "own system" of lies and trickery. He actually saw the mass murder of Americans as an encouraging sign, just when he needed one.

The conspirators' plans were roughly the same as before: Hitler would be assassinated. General Ludwig Beck, who had resigned in protest four years earlier, would lead the takeover. He would likely become the head of a new government. Beck "stood above all parties . . . [as] the only general with an [undamaged] reputation, the only general who had voluntarily resigned."[9] Having Beck as the leader of a new German government gave many other generals the courage to move forward.

For the first time, though, in February 1942, Dohnanyi learned that the Gestapo was watching him and Dietrich. Dohnanyi's telephone had been tapped, and his letters were being read. Aware of the increasing danger, Bonhoeffer drew up a will, which he gave to Bethge; he did not want to alarm his family. He knew he could be killed at any moment and wanted to make a plan in case he died. Eventually the Gestapo's watchfulness lessened, but they did not completely forget about Bonhoeffer and Dohnanyi.

THINK ABOUT IT

1. Why did Dietrich pretend to salute Hitler?
2. Why was working undercover as a spy a "very lonely place" for Bonhoeffer?
3. What did the Nazis think Bonhoeffer was doing in the Military Intelligence agency? What was he actually doing?
4. Bonhoeffer believed that if you do nothing to stop the bad things that you know are happening, then it's the same as if you were doing those bad things yourself. Do you agree? Why or why not?
5. Why did Bonhoeffer join the conspiracy against Hitler?

CHAPTER 12

MEETING MARIA

1942–1943

Why am I suddenly so cheerful these days? . . . The incredible fact remains, he actually wants to marry me. I still fail to grasp how that can be.

—MARIA VON WEDEMEYER

In the midst of widespread misery, one desires some happiness.

—DIETRICH BONHOEFFER

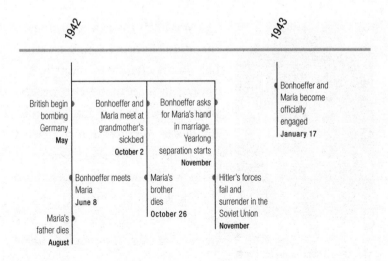

1942

British begin bombing Germany
May

Maria's father dies
August

Bonhoeffer meets Maria
June 8

Bonhoeffer and Maria meet at grandmother's sickbed
October 2

Maria's brother dies
October 26

Bonhoeffer asks for Maria's hand in marriage. Yearlong separation starts
November

Hitler's forces fail and surrender in the Soviet Union
November

1943

Bonhoeffer and Maria become officially engaged
January 17

On June 8, 1942, Bonhoeffer went to a village in northwest Germany to visit his dear friend, an older lady named **Ruth von Kleist-Retzow**. Her granddaughter **Maria von Wedemeyer** happened to be there. Maria recalled,

> [The] three of us got on extremely well together. The other two conversed in such a way that I not only felt I understood what they were talking about but was cordially encouraged to join in. Which I did.
>
> I'm afraid I used to take a cocky tone with my grandmother, which amused her, and which I maintained even when Dietrich turned up. We talked about future plans. Grandmother pronounced my plan to study mathematics a silly whim, but Dietrich, perhaps for that very reason, took it seriously.
>
> We went for a stroll in the garden. He said he'd been to America, and we noted with surprise that I'd never before met anyone who had been there.[1]

Art Resource

Maria von Wedemeyer, 1942

Maria left the next morning, so they didn't have much time together, but Bonhoeffer was smitten. As always, he needed time to process what he was feeling and thinking. But he was surprised at how affected he had been by the short time spent with this beautiful, intelligent, and confident young woman.

She was eighteen, and he was twice that age. Bonhoeffer knew

Maria's family well. Besides his longtime friendship with her grandmother, he had spent much time with her brother Max, who was two years older than Maria, and whom she adored. Max was then a lieutenant serving with the military. Bonhoeffer knew her parents too. There did not exist a couple more devoutly Christian—or more anti-Hitler.

Weeks later, Bonhoeffer spoke to Eberhard Bethge about Maria. As always, Bonhoeffer was trying to work out what he thought God was saying to him. On June 25, he wrote Bethge about his budding feelings:

> I have not written to Maria. It is truly not time for that yet. . . .
> I am in fact still not at all clear and decided about this.[2]

He did not see her all summer. But later that August, tragedy struck. Maria's father was killed in the war. He was fifty-four. Maria returned to her family immediately.

Maria's grandmother was in Berlin for an eye operation, and she had asked Maria to nurse her there. At the sickbed of her grandmother, she bumped into Dietrich again. Her thoughts toward him had not been the same as his toward her. And really, Bonhoeffer had not allowed his thoughts to get very far. But, in any case, he was at the hospital in the role of pastor, and Maria had just lost her father.

Years later, Maria recalled, "Dietrich's frequent visits [at the hospital] surprised me, and I was impressed by his devotion. We often had long talks together at this time. . . . Being still deeply affected by my father's death, I needed Dietrich's help."[3] They spent more time together than would have been possible under other circumstances.

LUNCH AT THE ALOIS

On one of Berlin's busiest squares was a restaurant and tea room called The Alois. It was named after the owner. Customers got a "Heil Hitler" salute from the waiters when they walked in the door, again when they got their menus, and again when they left. There were even portraits of Hitler hanging over the entrances. One day, Bonhoeffer invited Maria to lunch there since it was near the hospital. It was also one of the safest places they could talk freely. Why? It was owned by Hitler's brother, Alois Hitler! It was the last place anyone would think to find an anti-Hitler conspirator.[4]

Then on October 26, fresh tragedy struck. Maria's brother Max was killed in the war. Bonhoeffer wrote her with words of comfort: "'Weeping may endure for the night, but joy comes in the morning' (Psalm 30:5 NLT). There really is joy with God, with Christ! Do believe it."[5]

If ever there was a time to put aside thoughts of romance, this was it. Besides, it was only the beginning of a thought on Bonhoeffer's part. He made plans to come to Max's funeral and support the family. But Maria's grandmother had been watching them from her hospital bed for weeks—and she had other ideas. She thought there might be a spark developing between the two, and she foolishly mentioned this to her daughter.

Maria's mother was *not* happy. She sent Bonhoeffer a letter asking him not to come to the funeral. He was stunned. Maria's mother wrote that she felt her daughter was too young to be engaged to Pastor Bonhoeffer. Plus, a funeral was entirely the wrong time to think about these sorts of things. Bonhoeffer was shocked and horrified to think any of this could be out in the open.

Maria was blindsided by the whole thing. She wrote Bonhoeffer a letter saying that she had learned that her mother "had asked [Bonhoeffer] not to come for the memorial service, just because of some stupid family gossip which Grandmother has rather encouraged." As far as Maria was concerned, there was nothing to it, except that she was embarrassed.

When Bonhoeffer answered, he could not deny that he had feelings for her. He poured his words into a heartfelt apology for causing her and her family any anger or pain. But in this letter, in his ever-so-gentle way, Bonhoeffer hinted at a way forward:

> Only from a peaceful, free, healed heart can anything good and right take place; I have experienced that repeatedly in life, and I pray (forgive me for speaking thus) that God may grant us this, soon and very soon.
>
> Can you understand all this? Might you experience it just as I do? I hope so, in fact, I cannot conceive of anything else.
>
> . . . Please forgive me this letter, which says so clumsily what I am feeling . . . I will write to your mother tomorrow, that she not get upset at whatever your grandmother may be writing; the thought of it horrifies me.[6]

After a few more letters, Maria's mother asked him to stop writing her daughter. So Bonhoeffer sent an apology to Maria. He hinted that patience would be the only answer to the awkward situation: "So I ask it of God for you and for us and will wait until God shows us our way. Only in peace with God, with others, and with ourselves will we hear and do God's will. In this we may have great confidence and need not become impatient or act rashly."[7]

BONHOEFFER PROPOSES

The well-meaning grandmother's big mouth had let the cat out of the bag. Suddenly everything was out in the open. Then somehow, by later that November, Bonhoeffer had decided he wanted to marry Maria von Wedemeyer. He was going to ask her mother's permission to propose.

After he went to visit Mrs. von Wedemeyer, he wrote that she was "calm, friendly, and not [upset], as I had feared."[8] She was not completely against the match. But since it was such a big decision, and her daughter so young, she suggested a year of separation for Maria to think about it. Bonhoeffer was worried that a year might turn into longer, but he accepted the mother's decision.

CREATIVE COURTSHIP

For today's couples, not talking for a year might seem like an odd way to react to a marriage proposal. But it's far from the strangest thing to happen in courtship and dating around the world. Just consider some of these traditions:

- **Wales:** Since the 1600s, a man might spend hours carving a huge and elaborate "love spoon" to present to the lady who had caught his eye. If she accepted the spoon, she was willing to date him.

- **Victorian England:** If a girl were not interested in someone, she would rest her fan on her left cheek. If she were interested, she would rest it on her right cheek. Slow fanning meant she was already taken, while fast fanning meant she was looking for love.
- **New England:** In the 1700s, young men and ladies weren't allowed to be alone together without a family member in the room. There was no privacy for talking—until someone came up with the "courting stick." Couples used a hollow, six-foot-long stick to whisper to each other from across the room, without being overheard.
- **Austria:** Country girls in the 1800s would keep apple slices under their arms during dances. If a girl liked a guy, she would pull out her slice and present it to him. If he liked her back, he'd eat it.[9]

Maria's diary shows some of her feelings over that time:

Why am I suddenly so cheerful these days? . . . Ever since Mother told me on the phone about her meeting with Dietrich, I feel I can breathe freely again. He made a considerable impression on Mother, that's obvious—he couldn't fail to. The incredible fact remains, he actually wants to marry me. I still fail to grasp how that can be.[10]

Bonhoeffer had had no communication with Maria since November. But in early January she persuaded her mother and uncle to allow her to write Bonhoeffer. She wrote:

Dear Pastor Bonhoeffer,

I've known, ever since arriving home, that I must write to you, and I've looked forward to doing so. . . . [W]ords are so clumsy and forceful with things that want to be said gently. But because I have experienced that you understand me so well, I now have the courage to write you . . . Today I can say Yes to you from my entire, joyful heart. . . .

Yours, Maria[11]

Bonhoeffer wrote back immediately. For the first time he addressed her by her first name.

Dear Maria,

The letter was under way for four days before just now—an hour ago—arriving here! . . . May I simply say what is in my heart? I sense and am overwhelmed by the awareness that a gift without equal has been given me. . . . I want to speak to you as a man speaks to the girl with whom he wants to go through life and who has given him her Yes—dear Maria, I thank you for your word, for all that you have endured for me and for what you are and will be for me. Let us now be and become happy in each other. . . . I wish in no way to push or frighten you. I want to care for you and allow the dawning joy of our life to make you light and happy. . . . Let us [meet] each other in great, free forgiveness and love, let us take each other as we are—with thanks and boundless trust in God, who has led us to this point and now loves us.

This letter must be off immediately so that you will receive it tomorrow. God protect you and us both.

Your faithful Dietrich[12]

With that, Dietrich Bonhoeffer was engaged. They would look back on January 17 as the official date.

A LEGACY OF LOVE

Maria von Wedemeyer kept all her letters from Bonhoeffer. He wrote to her up until the end. But Maria wouldn't allow these letters to be published until she died. In 1977, she passed away, leaving a legacy of love behind her. Her letters from Dietrich, from 1943 to 1945, were made into a book, called *Love Letters from Cell 92.*

The couple still had to wait, but Bonhoeffer had much to keep him busy. Though he wasn't fully aware of it yet, the Gestapo was still on his tail. Meanwhile, the conspiracy was racing forward with yet another plan to kill Hitler.

When six days had passed and Bonhoeffer had not heard from Maria, he wrote again. His letter simply told her that all was well and that she should not feel rushed. The next day, Sunday the twenty-fourth, he received her letter. She asked him whether they might wait six months before they wrote again. It is thought that perhaps her mother had convinced her to ask this. It seemed to surprise Bonhoeffer, but he was too happy to be bothered by much. He was in love.

THINK ABOUT IT

1. Maria's grandmother unthinkingly caused trouble for Maria and Dietrich with her gossip. What does this tell you about gossip?

2. Why did Maria's mother want Maria and Bonhoeffer to wait so long before getting married?

3. How does Dietrich's response that they would "wait until God shows us our way" show wisdom?

4. Bonhoeffer respected Mrs. von Wedemeyer's decision, even though he didn't like it. Have your parents made decisions you didn't like?

5. What is the right way to respond to your parents' decisions?

CHAPTER 13

CELL 92

1943–1944

His soul really shone in the dark desperation of our prison . . .
[Bonhoeffer] had always been afraid that he would not be strong
enough to stand such a test but now he knew there was nothing in life
of which one need ever be afraid.

—CAPTAIN S. PAYNE BEST, BONHOEFFER'S FELLOW PRISONER, IN A
LETTER TO SABINE

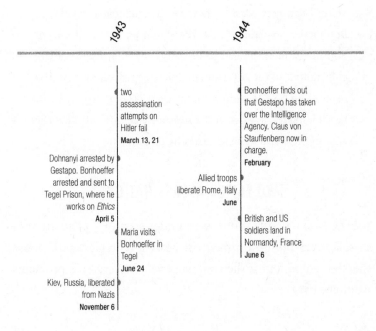

1943   1944

two
assassination
attempts on
Hitler fail
March 13, 21

Dohnanyi arrested by
Gestapo. Bonhoeffer
arrested and sent to
Tegel Prison, where he
works on *Ethics*
April 5

Maria visits
Bonhoeffer in
Tegel
June 24

Kiev, Russia, liberated
from Nazis
November 6

Bonhoeffer finds out
that Gestapo has taken
over the Intelligence
Agency. Claus von
Stauffenberg now in
charge.
February

Allied troops
liberate Rome, Italy
June

British and US
soldiers land in
Normandy, France
June 6

Maria's mother was not just concerned about Bonhoeffer's age; it was also his work for the German Military Intelligence agency. She might even have known of his involvement in the conspiracy. Indeed, the Gestapo had stumbled onto Bonhoeffer's trail the previous October when they brought in a fellow member of the agency and interrogated him. The agent surrendered information about Dohnanyi, Bonhoeffer, and others. Bonhoeffer knew that at any time he might be arrested and even killed. But he had already come to terms with that possibility.

One of Bonhoeffer's students remembered an extraordinary evening in November 1942, when they got into a conversation about whether it was right to kill Hitler. The student recalled:

> Suddenly [one of the guests] turned to Bonhoeffer and said: "Shall I shoot? I can get inside the Führer's headquarters with my revolver. I know where and when the conferences take place. I can get access." These words frightened us all. . . . Bonhoeffer explained that the shooting by itself meant nothing: something had to be gained by it, a change of circumstances, of the government. [Getting rid] of Hitler would in itself be no use; things might even become worse. That, he said, made the work of the resistance so difficult, that the "there-after" had to be so carefully prepared.[1]

TWO FAILED ASSASSINATIONS

All the while, preparations were under way for a coup attempt to take over the government in March. The Gestapo's noose was tightening, but if the coup succeeded, everyone's problems would be over.

But then on March 13 and again on March 21, 1943, two perfectly executed assassination attempts failed. Fortunately, the Nazis never found out about them. It was both disheartening and miraculous. The resistance had been foiled, but at least it had not been discovered.

FAILED ATTEMPTS

Hitler was a hard man to kill. There were more than forty documented attempts to assassinate him—and many more that weren't documented. Here are two clever plans from the resistance that didn't work:

- **Operation Flash: March 13, 1943.** Someone passed Hitler a bomb wrapped as a present for one of his officers. They expected it to go off while he was flying over Russia in a plane, but the bomb was defective and never exploded.
- **Memorial Day attempt: March 21, 1943.** Hitler was scheduled to visit a museum for a WWI memorial day dedication. A military officer was supposed to walk up to him with a bomb in each pocket and set them off. The trouble was, each bomb's fuse had to burn for ten minutes before exploding. The Führer only stayed at the memorial for eight minutes—not enough time for the bombs to go off. The plan was called off at the last minute.[2]

THE GESTAPO MAKE THEIR MOVE

On April 5, Bonhoeffer was at home. Around noon, he called the Dohnanyis' house. Their phone was answered by an unfamiliar man's voice. Bonhoeffer hung up. He knew what was happening: the Gestapo had finally made their move. Bonhoeffer calmly went next door to see his sister Ursula. He told her what had happened and that the Gestapo would likely arrest him too. She prepared a large meal for him, and then Bonhoeffer went back home to put his papers in order. The Gestapo would be searching his home, so he left a few fake notes designed to throw them off the conspiracy's trail.

Then Dietrich returned to his sister's and waited. At four o'clock Bonhoeffer's father came over and told him that two men wished to speak with him. They were upstairs in his room. Bonhoeffer met the Gestapo officials. Taking his Bible with him, he was escorted to their black car and taken away. He would never return.

Three months had passed between his engagement to Maria and his arrest. All the while, Bonhoeffer had respected her mother's wish that they not talk with each other. The day Dietrich was taken away, Maria felt a deep sense of dread. She wrote in her diary, "Has something bad happened? I'm afraid it's something very bad."[3] She had had no contact with Bonhoeffer or his family and had no idea that he had been arrested. A short time later, while Maria was visiting her uncle, she told him of her frustrations. He knew about Bonhoeffer's arrest and told her of it. Now it was too late to see him. For the rest of her life, Maria regretted not seeing him before he was arrested.

FIRST DAYS AT TEGEL

On the day Bonhoeffer was arrested, they also arrested Dohnanyi and their fellow conspirator, **Joseph Müller**. Bonhoeffer's sister

Christine Dohnanyi was arrested, too, as was Müller's wife. But only Bonhoeffer was taken to **Tegel military prison**.

Months later, Bonhoeffer wrote an account of his first days there:

> For the first night I was locked up in an admission cell. The blankets on the camp bed had such a foul smell that in spite of the cold it was impossible to use them. Next morning a piece of bread was thrown into my cell; I had to pick it up from the floor. A quarter of the coffee consisted of grounds. The sound of the prison staff's vile abuse of the prisoners who were held for investigation [drifted] into my cell for the first time; since then I have heard it every day from morning till night. When I had to parade with the other new arrivals, we were addressed by one of the jailers as "scoundrels," etc. etc. We were all asked why we had been arrested, and when I said I did not know the jailer answered with a scornful laugh, "You'll find that out soon enough."
>
> It was six months before I got a warrant for my arrest. . . . I was taken to the most isolated cell on the top floor; a notice, [forbidding] all access without special permission, was put outside it. I was told that all my [letters] would be stopped until further notice and that, unlike all the other prisoners, I should not be allowed half an hour a day in the open air, although, according to the prison rules, I was entitled to it. . . . After forty-eight hours my Bible was returned to me; it had been searched to see whether I had smuggled inside it a saw, razor blades, or the like. For the next twelve days the cell door was opened only for bringing food in and putting the bucket out. No one said a word to me. I was told nothing about the

reason for my [arrest], or how long it would last. I gathered
from various remarks—and it was confirmed later—that I
was lodged in the section for the most serious cases, where
the condemned prisoners lay shackled.[4]

For the first twelve days Bonhoeffer was treated as a serious
criminal. The cells around him held men sentenced to death—
one of whom wept through Bonhoeffer's first night, making sleep
impossible. On the cell wall Bonhoeffer read a scrawled message
from a former prisoner: "In a hundred years it'll all be over."[5]

From the beginning of his imprisonment, Bonhoeffer maintained the daily disciplines of scriptural meditation and prayer.
Once he got his Bible back, he read it for hours each day. By
November he had read through the Old Testament two and a
half times.

Eventually, Dietrich was moved to cell 92—"a cell looking
south with a sweeping view across the prison yard to the pine
forest."[6] It featured a plank bed, a bench along one wall, a stool,
and a bucket to use for a toilet. There was a wooden door with
a tiny circular window through which the guards might look in
on him. A not-so-small window above his head provided daylight and fresh air. It might have been worse. Bonhoeffer's family
lived seven miles south and visited often, providing him with
food, clothing, books, and other things.

At first he was allowed only one letter every ten days, and
these letters could be only one page. This frustrated him terribly.
But Bonhoeffer quickly became friendly with some of the guards,
who were able to sneak other letters out for him. And so a flood
of letters began. Between November 1943 and August 1944,
Bonhoeffer wrote two hundred very crowded pages to his friend

Eberhard Bethge alone. His parents would send small gifts of all kinds, including flowers for his birthday, as would Maria. She even brought him a huge Christmas tree in December, though it was too large to put in his cell and had to be set up in the guards' room.

But Bonhoeffer's attitude did not depend on these comforts. His first letter home painted a picture of all that was going on inside him:

> Dear Parents! I do want you to be quite sure that I'm all right. I'm sorry that I was not allowed to write to you sooner, but I was all right during the first ten days too. Strangely enough, the discomforts that one generally associates with prison life, the physical hardships, hardly bother me at all.[7]

This letter and many of the letters he wrote were read by **Manfred Roeder**, the man prosecuting him. Bonhoeffer was writing on two levels: on one level to his parents, but on another to the hostile set of eyes belonging to the Nazis reading through everything he wrote, searching for evidence against him. Dietrich was feeding Roeder the information he wanted him to have through his letters. Most importantly, he wanted Roeder to think that he knew nothing about the plan to kill Hitler.

CAT AND MOUSE

Bonhoeffer and the others knew the Nazis didn't have a clue about the conspiracy against Hitler. So they continued their games of deception, even though some of their leaders were behind bars. They knew that any moment Hitler could be assassinated and they could be set free.

The Bonhoeffer family had always been good at understanding the hidden meanings behind words. Now, as Dietrich would write letters home, he knew that they would be read and understood on two levels. His parents would be able to tell he was writing certain things to fool Roeder. He trusted them to be able to separate out what was meant for them and what was meant for Roeder.

The family had also worked out ahead of time how to communicate if any of them were put in prison. One method was to put coded messages in the books they were allowed to pass back and forth. Bonhoeffer got many books from his parents and would send them back when he was finished with them. To signal that there was a coded message in the book, they would underline the name of the book's owner on the front page or inside cover. So, if *D. Bonhoeffer* was underlined, they knew there was a message from him inside.

The message itself was given through a series of the tiniest pencil marks under letters on pages in the book. Every three or every ten pages—the number seemed to vary—a light pencil dot would be put under a letter on that page. A set number of pages later another letter would be marked with a dot. These marks would begin at the back of the book and go toward the front. So a three-hundred-page book might have room for a thirty-letter message.

BREAK THE CODE

Can you use the code the Bonhoeffers used? Read this prayer Dietrich wrote in prison, and work back to front to collect bold letters and decode the secret message.

And, if you're up for more of a challenge, flip through this book from front to back and find the letters marked with a dot under them. What message do you find?

O God, early in the morning I cry to you. Help me to pray and gather my thoughts to you, I cannot do it alone. In me it is dark, but with you there is light; I am lonely, but you do not desert me; my courage fails me, but with you there is help; I am restless, but with you there is peace; in me there is bitterness, but with you there is patience; I do not understand your ways, but you know the way for me. Father in Heaven, praise and thanks be to you for the night's rest. Praise and thanks be to you for the new day. Praise and thanks be to you for all your loving-kindness and faithfulness in my past life. You have shown me so much goodness; let me also accept what is hard to bear from your hand. You will not lay a heavier burden on me than I can carry. You make all things serve for the best for your children. Lord, whatever this day brings, your name be praised.

ANSWER: Courage in faith. For the answer to the full book code, see page 242.

These were usually extremely important and dangerous messages. Some messages were about what Dohnanyi had told his interrogator, so that Bonhoeffer could back up that information. This prevented Dietrich from getting tripped up or caught saying something different than Dohnanyi had said.

Younger members of the Bonhoeffer family often had the task of looking for the barely visible pencil markings. Their younger eyes were much better at seeing them on the page. Christopher von Dohnanyi, Dietrich's nephew, recalled another way they were able to slip messages past the Nazis: "You could take a glass for jam or marmalade . . . there was a double lid. The lid had a double cardboard. Between this cardboard and the metal, my mother and we would cut little rounds, and there we would write the most dangerous things!"[8] Hans von Dohnanyi wrote entire letters in miniature script on this secret stationery.

IRENA SENDLER, SMUGGLER OF CHILDREN

It was dangerous to smuggle messages to prisoners during these hard times. But even more dangerous and daring was the smuggling of people.

A Polish social worker named Irena Sendler saved more than 2,500 Jewish children in Warsaw, Poland. Her work took her into the Warsaw ghetto where the Jews were held prisoner. Here are a few of the ways she and her organization smuggled children to safety:

- wrapped up as packages
- carried out in the bottom of a tool box
- in sacks
- in suitcases
- in the back of ambulances or trams
- in boxes in the back of a truck

Older kids disguised themselves as laborers going out to work in the town. Sometimes they were smuggled out through secret passages. Irena and her organization gave each child a new name and a new home with a Catholic family, an orphanage, or a convent until the danger passed. She wrote down the real name of every child they smuggled out on small slips of paper. She buried the papers in a jar in her neighbor's backyard. After the war was over, she dug it up and tried to help those 2,500 children find their families—though most had died in concentration camps. She was nominated for a Nobel Peace Prize for her bravery, but said, "The term 'hero' irritates me greatly. The opposite is true. I continue to have pangs of conscience that I did so little."[9]

Throughout his eighteen months at Tegel prison, Bonhoeffer posed as a simple and idealistic pastor, not at all involved with political issues. He played dumb brilliantly, both in the interrogations and in the often long letters that he wrote to Roeder: "I am the last person to deny that I might have made mistakes in work so strange, so new and so complicated as that of the [Military Intelligence agency]. I often find it hard to follow the speed of your questions, probably because I am not used to them."[10]

But Bonhoeffer had another advantage at Tegel prison. His uncle **Paul von Hase** was the military officer in charge of Berlin. That made him the big boss, high above the top warden at Tegel prison. When the guards at Tegel learned of this, everything changed. It was as if they had a celebrity in their midst. Dietrich's fame was not only because of his uncle, but also because of the great mystery that surrounded his imprisonment. He was a pastor and quite clearly an enemy of the Nazi state. But many of the guards were quietly against the Nazis too. And as they got to know Dietrich, they found him genuinely kind and generous, even to those guards the others hated.

KEEPING BUSY IN PRISON

Bonhoeffer was soon given privileges in the prison. Sometimes it was because of who his uncle was, but more often it was because of his good attitude. Others found him to be a source of comfort to them and wanted him around while they were stuck in the gloom of the prison. They wished to speak with him, to tell him their problems, to confess things to him, and simply to be near him.

A LIGHT IN THE DARKNESS

People couldn't help wanting to be around Bonhoeffer. It wasn't because he was popular or cool or funny. And it wasn't because of his looks or his talents. Those things didn't really matter. It was because he had the light of God shining through him, like a warm lamp in the cold and dark prison. How can you be a light in the dark?

- Don't be afraid. God loves and protects you, so you don't have to worry about what's going on around you.
- Be kind to everyone—no matter who they are, no matter who doesn't like them. Everyone needs God's light.
- Be a good listener. Sometimes listening is more important than talking.
- Don't run away from people who are having a hard time. Visit them, sit with them, and be a positive force in their lives. A "fair-weather friend" is someone who is only around when everything is fun and nice. A true friend sticks around through the bad times as well as the good times.

- Pray for those around you. In his book *Life Together*, Bonhoeffer said, "I can no longer condemn or hate a brother for whom I pray, no matter how much trouble he causes me."

While in prison, Bonhoeffer still did an impressive amount of reading and writing. Most especially, he worked on his book *Ethics*. Bonhoeffer thought of *Ethics* as his greatest work. It was the book that he never quite finished. He had worked on it for years, all across Germany, wherever he lived. The book opens with these lines:

[Christians] must give up . . . the very two questions that led them to deal with the ethical problem: "How can I be good?" and "How can I do something good?" Instead they must ask the wholly other, completely different question: "What is the will of God?" . . . All things appear as in a [warped] mirror if they are not seen and recognized in God.[11]

BONHOEFFER'S BOOKS: *ETHICS*

Bonhoeffer never finished writing his book *Ethics*, but his best friend Eberhard Bethge finished it for him. In *Ethics* Bonhoeffer wrote about:

- telling the truth
- government responsibility
- God's commandments
- conscience
- freedom
- responsibility

- talents and calling
- justice

- shame
- conflicts

Bonhoeffer said,

> Do and dare what is right, not swayed by the whim of the moment. Bravely take hold of the real, not dallying now with what might be. Not in the flight of ideas but only in action is freedom. Make up your mind and come out into the tempest of living. God's command is enough and your faith in him to sustain you. Then at last freedom will welcome your spirit amid great rejoicing.[12]

LOVE LETTERS FROM CELL 92

Bonhoeffer's relationship with Maria was a source of strength and hope for him in prison. When she learned of his arrest, Bonhoeffer's future mother-in-law allowed the engagement to be made public. Dietrich was very grateful for this kindness. It gave him and Maria more hope that their future together was a reality, soon to come. Everyone was convinced Bonhoeffer would be released quite soon, once the Nazi investigator Roeder got his questions answered.

In the meantime, on May 23, Maria visited his parents in Berlin, where she was received as Dietrich's fiancée. She wrote to him:

My dear, dear Dietrich,

You thought of me yesterday, didn't you? I sense how constantly you were at my side, how you went with me through all those unfamiliar rooms to meet all those people, and how everything suddenly seemed familiar, homely, and very dear. I'm so happy about that day in Berlin, Dietrich . . . I like your parents. The moment your mother greeted me I knew I couldn't fail to . . . Oh, I fell in love with everything. Your house, the garden, and—most of all—your room. . . . I never thought I could miss you and long for you more than I do, but I've done so twice as much since yesterday.

. . . My dearest Dietrich, every morning at six, when we both fold our hands in prayer, we know that we can have great faith, not only in each other but far, far above and beyond that. And then you can't be sad any more either, can you? I'll write again soon.

Whatever I think or do, I'm always

Your Maria[13]

Maria and Dietrich began writing back and forth, making wedding plans and deciding on hymns and honeymoons. She was given permission to visit on June 24, although Bonhoeffer did not know she would be coming. Roeder surprised him by bringing Maria into the room. Maria wrote years later, "I was brought into the room with practically no forewarning, and Dietrich was visibly shaken. He first reacted with silence, but then carried on a normal conversation; his emotions showed only in the pressure with which he held my hand."[14]

When their time together was over, Roeder took Maria in one direction, while Bonhoeffer had to leave by another door.

But just as Maria was about to leave the room, she showed the independent spirit and strong will for which she was famous: against the wishes of Roeder, she ran back across the room and hugged her fiancé one last time, much to Roeder's irritation. This would be the first of seventeen visits. Their hopes for an early trial and release were very much alive, and they were constantly thinking about their upcoming marriage.

In October, Bonhoeffer had been in prison at Tegel for six months. On November 26, 1943, he was given the unique treat of a visit from the four people in the world he loved most: Maria, his parents, and Eberhard Bethge. They came together, and when Bonhoeffer returned to his cell, he was beside himself:

> It will be with me for a long time now—the memory of having the four people who are nearest and dearest to me with me for a brief moment. When I got back to my cell afterwards, I paced up and down for a whole hour, while my dinner stood there and got cold, so that at last I couldn't help laughing at myself when I found myself repeating over and over again, "That was really great!" I always hesitate to use the word "indescribable" about anything, because if you take enough trouble to make a thing clear, I think there is very little that is really "indescribable"—but at the moment that is just what this morning seems to be.[15]

On February 4, 1944, his thirty-eighth birthday, Bonhoeffer received another visit from Maria, who unknowingly brought some hard news. One of the books she passed along to him that day contained a coded message from his parents: the Gestapo had taken over the Military Intelligence agency. Admiral Canaris, who had been a leader in the conspiracy to assassinate Hitler, was out. But all hope was not lost. Over the following months, a new group of conspirators emerged. It was led by a man named **Colonel Claus von Stauffenberg.**

THINK ABOUT IT

1. How was it possible for Dietrich to be happy in prison?
2. Why did the guards and other prisoners at Tegel seem to like Dietrich?
3. When people were running from the Gestapo, they were often sheltered by others who risked their lives to hide them. Have you ever risked something to help someone else? Have you ever risked . . .
   - your reputation?
   - your things?
   - your time?
   - doing what you wanted to do?

CHAPTER 14

THE CONSPIRACY FAILS

1944–1945

A human being's moral integrity begins when he is prepared to sacrifice his life for his convictions.

—HENNING VON TRESCKOW

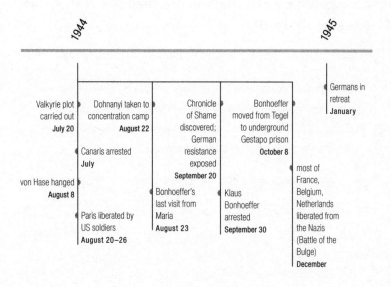

				Germans in retreat **January**
Valkyrie plot carried out **July 20**	Dohnanyi taken to concentration camp **August 22**	Chronicle of Shame discovered; German resistance exposed **September 20**	Bonhoeffer moved from Tegel to underground Gestapo prison **October 8**	
	Canaris arrested **July**			most of France, Belgium, Netherlands liberated from the Nazis (Battle of the Bulge) **December**
von Hase hanged **August 8**		Bonhoeffer's last visit from Maria **August 23**	Klaus Bonhoeffer arrested **September 30**	
	Paris liberated by US soldiers **August 20–26**			

On June 30, 1944, Paul von Hase, the military commandant of Berlin, entered the gates of Tegel prison. His purpose? To see his nephew—the prisoner in cell 92, Dietrich Bonhoeffer. It was almost as if Hitler himself had suddenly shown up for lunch. Bonhoeffer wrote Bethge that it was "most comical how everyone goes about flapping his wings and—with a few notable exceptions—tries to outdo everyone else in undignified ways."[1] Incredibly, von Hase stayed for more than five hours, visiting and relaxing with Dietrich. His uncle had dared to take sides— *against* the Nazis and *with* his nephew.

His uncle's bold appearance suggested that the government takeover was coming soon. It signaled to Bonhoeffer that Hitler would soon be dead, and they could all begin life again. Bonhoeffer already knew things were in motion, but his uncle's visit strongly confirmed it. His uncle, von Hase, was not just aware of the conspiracy; he was a key part of it. The plans for this latest plot had been in place for a year, but there had never been a good time to carry them out. Until now. The plot was code-named **Valkyrie**.

The Valkyries are characters in old Norse mythology. They are women who chose which warriors were worthy to be honored after death, and they protected the lives of the warriors they loved. *The Valkyrie* was also the title of one of Hitler's favorite operas.[2]

COLONEL VON STAUFFENBERG:
A MAN WITH A MISSION

Colonel Claus von Stauffenberg could have allowed all sorts of things to stop him from taking on the dangerous Valkyrie mission. For one, he had suffered terrible injuries during the war:

- He wore an eye patch because he had lost an eye.
- He had lost his right hand.
- He only had three fingers on his left hand.
- He had to dress himself using his teeth.

But while he was healing from his injuries, Stauffenberg built up his courage and his resolve. His bravery beat all his physical limitations.[3]

The final and famous plot against Hitler would be led by Colonel Claus von Stauffenberg, a devout Catholic from an aristocratic family. In late 1943 he told a fellow conspirator, "Let's get to the heart of the matter: I am committing high treason with all my might and main."

On July 19, Stauffenberg was ordered to be at **Wolfsschanze**, or the "Wolf's Lair," Hitler's headquarters on the eastern front. It was a secure fortress compound, tucked away in a remote forest. Stauffenberg was to be there the next day for a one o'clock meeting. He knew this was the chance for which he had been patiently waiting.

The next morning, on July 20, he arose at five. He drove to the airport with his assistant, who had spoken for hours to

Bonhoeffer about killing the Führer. With them was Stauffenberg's briefcase. The briefcase held important papers and—wrapped carefully in a shirt—a plastic bomb. They stopped at a Catholic chapel where Stauffenberg went inside to pray.

After a three-hour plane ride, Stauffenberg and his assistant were picked up by a staff car and driven through the gloomy woods surrounding Hitler's headquarters. Just before twelve thirty, Stauffenberg asked if he could change his shirt. When alone, he quickly opened his briefcase, unwrapped the bomb, put on the shirt in which it was wrapped, and set the bomb, placing it back in the briefcase. It would explode in ten minutes.

By the time Stauffenberg entered the room where Hitler was meeting, four of the ten minutes had ticked away. Hitler briefly greeted Stauffenberg, who took his place near the Führer, placing the briefcase and its bomb under the massive oak table at which they all sat. It was just six feet from the Führer's legs.

Suddenly, the great oak table was in smithereens. Hair was on fire. The ceiling had collapsed onto the floor. Several men lay dead. But Hitler was fine and dandy, albeit a little flustered. "It was Providence that spared me," Hitler later declared. "This proves that I'm on the right track. I feel that this is the confirmation of all my work."[4]

A radio microphone was rigged up around midnight, and all Germany heard the voice of the Führer:

> If I speak to you today, I do so for two special reasons. In
> the first place, so that you may hear my voice and know that
> I myself am sound and uninjured; and in the second place,

so that you may also hear the particulars about a crime that is without [equal] in German history. An extremely small clique of ambitious, conscienceless, and criminal and stupid officers forged a plot to eliminate me [and my officers]. The bomb, which was planted by Colonel Count von Stauffenberg, burst two yards from my right side. It injured several of my colleagues; one of them has died. I myself am wholly unhurt. . . . I see in this another sign from Providence that I must and therefore shall continue my work.[5]

The blow to Hitler's pride must have been shattering, and he wouldn't stand for it. He would wipe out every trace of opposition and torture information from any possible source. The wives, children, family members, and friends of anyone connected to this conspiracy would be hunted down, arrested, and sent to concentration camps. The end of the conspiracy had begun.

THE WOLF'S LAIR

The name Adolf comes from an old German word *Adelwolf,* meaning "noble wolf." Hitler adopted the symbol of the wolf as his own. In the 1920s he sometimes registered at hotels as Herr (Mr.) Wolf. He named his military headquarters during the Battle of France *Wolfsschlucht* (Wolf's Gorge) and the command post on the eastern front *Werwolf* (Werewolf). But the most famous of his wolfish haunts was the bunker where Stauffenberg's Valkyrie plot failed *Wolfsschanze* (Wolf's Lair).

AFTERMATH

Bonhoeffer heard the news of the failed assassination attempt while listening to the radio during a visit to the sick bay at Tegel. He knew what the consequences would be. Days later he heard that Admiral Canaris, the old leader of the Military Intelligence agency, had been arrested. He would soon hear more. Stauffenberg's assistant had died bravely, leaping into a wave of bullets intended for Stauffenberg. Stauffenberg died bravely, too, just moments later. Just before being executed, he shouted, "Long live sacred Germany!"[6]

One of the executed conspirators said this before he died:

> The whole world will [criticize] us now, but I am still totally convinced that we did the right thing. Hitler is the archenemy not only of Germany but of the world. When, in a few hours' time, I go before God to account for what I have done and left undone, I know I will be able to justify in good conscience what I did in the struggle against Hitler. . . . A human being's moral integrity begins when he is prepared to sacrifice his life for his convictions.[7]

Everyone remotely connected to the conspiracy was arrested and interrogated. Most were tortured. The Nazis would do anything to get information out of them.

interrogate

(in-'ter-ə-gāt): to question formally and thoroughly[8]

The purpose of interrogation is to find out the truth. Good interrogators use calm and clever logic to get a person to reveal the truth. But the Nazis often used violence and cruelty to force prisoners to give them the information they wanted.

On August 8, Bonhoeffer's uncle, General Paul von Hase, was sentenced to death and hanged that same day. He was fifty-nine years old. His wife was arrested, and so were the spouses and relatives of many in the conspiracy. On August 22, Hans von Dohnanyi was taken to Sachsenhausen concentration camp. On September 20, the Chronicle of Shame files he had been keeping were discovered in the town of Zossen, where they had been hidden. For Bonhoeffer and Dohnanyi, this was the disaster of disasters. Dohnanyi had been keeping those files since 1938, collecting evidence of the criminal horrors of the Nazis. Their discovery would bring the whole conspiracy out into the light, and they knew it. Their secret was out.

MARIA LOSES HOPE

Even in the months before the failed July 20 assassination attempt, there were signs from Maria that all the waiting and stress was becoming hard to bear. She began suffering from headaches, sleeplessness, and even fainting fits. In mid-August, she decided to move in with Dietrich's parents and help them at their home in Berlin. She would also be closer to Dietrich there. Maria visited Bonhoeffer again on August 23. As things turned out, it would be the last time they ever saw each other. Bonhoeffer wrote to Bethge that day: "Maria was here today, so fresh and at the same time steadfast . . . in a way I've rarely seen."[9]

THE GESTAPO PRISON

On Saturday, September 30, Dietrich's brother Klaus saw a car parked near his house. The sight of it caused him to turn around immediately and drive away. Klaus was sure it was a Gestapo car. If he had gone home, he would have been arrested and taken away. So he drove to his sister Ursula's house, where he stayed overnight. The next morning, Sunday, the Gestapo arrived at Ursula's home and took Klaus away. Now two Bonhoeffer brothers were imprisoned.

The following Sunday, October 8, 1944, Bonhoeffer's eighteen months at Tegel prison came to an end. He was secretly moved to another Gestapo prison—this one much worse. The cells were underground. He had no opportunity to see the light of day. There was no prison yard to walk in, no birds to hear sing, and no friendly guards.

When Bonhoeffer was first interrogated by the Gestapo, he was threatened with torture. He was told that the fate of his parents, his other family members, and his fiancée depended upon his confession. Nothing leads us to believe he was ever tortured, but his brother Klaus and most of the other conspirators were.

Getty Images

Tegel military prison in Berlin, where Bonhoeffer was held for eighteen months before his transfer to the underground Gestapo prison. The "x" marks the cell where he first stayed. He was later transferred to Cell 92 on the third floor.

THE WAR WINDS DOWN

By the time Bonhoeffer left Tegel prison in October 1944, the Nazis suspected they were losing the war.

- June 6, D-Day: the Allies invade France to take it back from the Nazis
- July 17: first Russian units get to Poland
- August 15: Hitler's forces begin retreating out of France
- August 25: Allies free Paris from Nazi control
- September 3–5: Belgium is freed from Nazi control
- September 11: the United States Army steps into Germany[10]

Bonhoeffer could no longer write to Maria. She made the trek to the prison a number of times, hoping to be allowed to visit. Each time she was denied. But the war was winding down, and things were not going well for Germany. Finally, the prison guards allowed Bonhoeffer to write Maria at Christmas:

19 December 1944
My dearest Maria,

I'm so glad to be able to write you a Christmas letter, and to be able, through you, to convey my love to my parents and my brothers and sisters, to thank you all. Our homes will be very quiet at this time. But . . . I haven't for an instant felt lonely and forlorn. You yourself, my parents . . . are my constant companions. Your prayers and kind thoughts, passages from the Bible, long-forgotten conversations, pieces of music, books—all are invested with life and reality as never before. . . . So you mustn't think I'm unhappy. Anyway, what do happiness and unhappiness mean? They depend so little on circumstances and so much more on what goes on inside us. I'm thankful every day to have you—you and all of you—and that makes me happy and cheerful. . . .

We've now been waiting for each other for almost two years, dearest Maria. Don't lose heart! I'm glad you're with my parents. Give my fondest love to our mother and the whole family. . . . In great love and gratitude to you, my parents, and my brothers and sisters.

I embrace you.

Yours, Dietrich[11]

THINK ABOUT IT

1. Hitler adopted the symbol of the wolf as his own. How were his personality and his actions like that of a wolf?
2. Bonhoeffer said happiness depends on what's happening inside, rather than outside. Has there been a time when you've been unhappy because of your circumstances (things happening on the outside)?
3. How can you be happy on the inside, even when things are going badly on the outside?

CHAPTER 15

ON THE ROAD TO FREEDOM

1945

[Christians] must not fear men. Men can do them no harm, for the power of men [ends] with the death of the body. But they must overcome the fear of death with the fear of God.

—DIETRICH BONHOEFFER

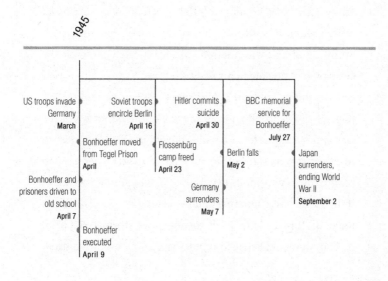

1945

US troops invade Germany
March

Bonhoeffer and prisoners driven to old school
April 7

Soviet troops encircle Berlin
April 16

Bonhoeffer moved from Tegel Prison
April

Bonhoeffer executed
April 9

Hitler commits suicide
April 30

Flossenbürg camp freed
April 23

Germany surrenders
May 7

BBC memorial service for Bonhoeffer
July 27

Berlin falls
May 2

Japan surrenders, ending World War II
September 2

From this point on, the information on Bonhoeffer becomes scarce. Most of what we know about him during this four-month period comes from Maria's cousin, who was in prison with him for a time. Some of his account reads this way:

> I must admit that I was filled with alarm when I caught sight of Dietrich Bonhoeffer. But when I saw his upright figure and his [peaceful] glance, I took comfort, and I knew that he had recognized me without losing his composure. . . . The very next morning I was able to have a word with him [secretly] in the washroom . . . Dietrich let me know immediately that he was determined to resist all the efforts of the Gestapo, and to reveal nothing . . . Dietrich Bonhoeffer told me of his interrogations. . . . His noble and pure soul must have suffered deeply. But he betrayed no sign of it. He was always good-tempered, always of the same kindliness and politeness towards everybody, so that to my surprise, within a short time, he had won over his warders, who were not always kindly disposed. . . . Many little notes he slipped into my hands on which he had written biblical words of comfort and hope. He looked with optimism at his own situation too. He repeatedly told me the Gestapo had no clue to his real activities. . . .
>
> On the morning of 3rd February 1945 an air raid turned the city of Berlin into a heap of rubble; the buildings of the Gestapo Headquarters were also burnt out. Tightly squeezed together we were standing in our air-raid shelter when a bomb hit it with an enormous explosion. For a second it seemed as if the shelter were bursting and the ceiling crashing down on top of us. It rocked like a ship tossing in the storm, but it held. At that moment Dietrich Bonhoeffer showed his [strength of

spirit.] He remained quite calm, he did not move a muscle, but stood motionless and relaxed as if nothing had happened.

On 7th February 1945 in the morning I spoke to him for the last time. On the same day around noon the number of his cell was called up amongst others. The prisoners were divided into two groups. Bonhoeffer was transported to Buchenwald, the concentration camp near Weimar.[1]

WORDS OF COMFORT AND HOPE

Dietrich passed people little notes to comfort them. Written on some of them were words from the Bible.

People always need words of comfort and hope, even when they're not in prison. Today, find four small pieces of paper, and write notes of encouragement to your friends, family, or even people you don't know that well. Especially seek out those people who are going through a difficult time.

If you want to write words of hope from the Bible, here are a few:

- We know that in everything God works for the good of those who love him. (Romans 8:28 NCV)
- The LORD . . . will be with you; he will not leave you or forget you. Don't be afraid and don't worry. (Deuteronomy 31:8 NCV)
- I know what I am planning for you," says the LORD. "I have good plans for you, not plans to hurt you. I will give you hope and a good future. (Jeremiah 29:11 NCV)

BUCHENWALD CONCENTRATION CAMP

In the early afternoon of February 7, Bonhoeffer and a number of other important prisoners were taken from their cells. They were made to wait near two vans that would take them to the concentration camps at Buchenwald and Flossenbürg. There were twenty men, all major players in the conspiracy.

Bonhoeffer had just celebrated his thirty-ninth birthday in a Gestapo cell and now saw his first daylight in four months. For most of the prisoners, it had been far longer. Wherever they were headed, to be outdoors together lifted everyone's spirits. It was clear the war was ending and Hitler was finished.

Now they would take a long journey, two hundred miles south to Buchenwald, which was one of the Nazi centers of death. But it was not just a place where people died; it was a place where death was celebrated. Buchenwald and the other camps like it throughout the Third Reich were living examples of the satanic worldview of the SS. In these places, weakness was preyed upon, and millions of people were cruelly abused and killed.

CONCENTRATION CAMPS

The Nazis built concentration camps and death camps all over the territories that they conquered. There, they would imprison Jews, Roma gypsies, people who spoke out against them, and many other "undesirables."

The term *concentration camp* came from the fact that large numbers of people were "concentrated," or collected, in one place. The people were forced to work like slaves. Men were separated from women, and children were separated from their families. Most died of disease or starvation . . . or murder.

Death camps—or "death factories"—were set up for one reason: to kill people. Most often, the camps used gas chambers to kill. The Nazi guards would line people up to go to "bath houses" to take showers. But instead of water, poison gas would spray out of the faucets. There was no escape. At one camp, as many as two thousand could be gassed each hour. Other prisoners were shot, and still others were hanged. These camps were supposed to be secret, so the Nazis often destroyed the bodies by burning them in huge ovens. By the end of the war, almost three million people had been killed in these death camps.

The Buchenwald death camp specialized in killing people in particularly horrible ways. Doctors did gruesome experiments on the prisoners, not caring if they lived or died. Buchenwald also held political prisoners—those people who disagreed with the government. That is why Dietrich Bonhoeffer was taken there.[2]

THE HOLOCAUST

The **Holocaust** was a time of horror and bloodshed on a massive scale. It was the organized killing of over six million Jewish men, women, and children, along with millions of people. These terrible crimes were carried out by the Nazis and their allies during World War II.

The word *Holocaust* comes from the Greek *holokauston*, meaning "a burnt sacrifice." This word was chosen because in the death camps, the bodies of the victims were disposed of by burning them in ovens or open fires.

In 1933, there were about nine million Jews in Europe. By the time the war ended, two out of every three Jews had been killed. One and a half million of them were children.[3]

Bonhoeffer spent seven weeks at Buchenwald concentration camp. He was not in the main camp, but just outside it in a cold prison cellar that had previously been used as a military jail for the SS. Now it would hold seventeen rather remarkable prisoners. They were considered special because of their rank and position in society.

We have no letters from Bonhoeffer during this period, but one of the men he met at Buchenwald was the British intelligence officer Captain S. Payne Best. He wrote an account of their time together at Buchenwald in his autobiography. Best arrived there on February 24, with three other prisoners. One was another British officer, Hugh Falconer; the second was a soviet air force officer, Vassily Kokorin; and the third was General Friedrich von Rabenau, who joined Bonhoeffer in his small cell.

The sixty-year-old General Rabenau was a Christian whose faith had led him to speak out against Hitler early on. Rabenau and Bonhoeffer spent hours talking about theology and playing chess.

Captain Best described Bonhoeffer as "all humility and sweetness; he always seemed to me to diffuse an atmosphere of happiness, of joy in every smallest event in life, and of deep gratitude for the mere fact that he was alive. . . . He was one of the very few men that I have ever met to whom his God was real and ever close to him."[4]

Bonhoeffer and everyone else hung on in the cold and

hunger, knowing that any moment they might be either set free or killed. Then on April 1, Easter Sunday, the thunder of the American guns could be heard in the distance. It would all be over soon, they thought. But sometime later that day the chief guard told the prisoners to get ready to leave.

Hours passed, then days. At ten on Tuesday evening, word came. The prisoners would not have to travel on foot, but the van that would carry them was designed for eight people without luggage. There were sixteen people, and they all had luggage. Also, the van was fueled by wood fed into a generator, and once under way, the passenger area became filled with choking wood smoke. Nonetheless, they were leaving Buchenwald.

FACT: The Americans freed the prisoners of Buchenwald on April 12, 1945. Bonhoeffer had been moved just nine days before that.

JOURNEY INTO THE UNKNOWN

The sixteen prisoners—an oddball crew by any standard—crammed themselves into the van along with their luggage. It was quite a cast of characters: aristocratic army generals, a naval commander, a diplomat and his wife, a depressed Russian air force officer, a Catholic lawyer, a theologian, a woman accused of being a spy, and a concentration camp "doctor." They left sometime after ten and traveled through the night, chugging along at fifteen miles per hour. They only covered eight or nine miles every hour because they had to keep stopping to clean the wood-burning engine and restock it with wood.

THE DREADFUL DR. RASCHER

One of the men in Bonhoeffer's van was Sigmund Rascher, a Nazi concentration camp doctor. But far from helping people, he used his skills to hurt and kill. He was the man who had designed the gas chambers that were used to murder millions in the death camps. But he had offended the Nazi government and was now a prisoner himself.

Rascher also knew about "gas wagons" or "gas vans"—mobile gas chambers in the backs of vans. When the van they were riding in filled with wood smoke, he exclaimed in fear, "My God, this is a death van; we are being gassed!"

Though some of the people in the van fainted, in the end the smoke escaped from a vent, and they continued on their journey.[5]

After thirteen hours of this sort of travel, it was noon the next day. They had reached a small town in northern Bavaria. About ten miles east lay the concentration camp of Flossenbürg. In the town, they stopped at the police station, and the guards went in. Upon returning, the friendliest of the three guards told his captives: "You will have to go farther. They can't take you here. Too full."[6] But what did that mean? Dr. Rascher—the concentration camp "expert"—explained that if they were to be killed, Flossenbürg would have made room for them. The camp was only too full for living prisoners. So this was good news. It seemed they wouldn't be killed that day.

The guards got back in, and they continued traveling. Just as they reached the edge of town, a car passed them and motioned for them to pull over. Two policemen stepped out. What happened next is unclear, but it seems they had room for three of the prisoners at Flossenbürg, after all. Three of the men said good-bye to their fellow prisoners and went with the policemen. It was now Wednesday afternoon, April 4. Captain Best wrote:

> After leaving [the town] there was a marked change in the attitude of the three SS guards. They had obviously left Buchenwald with orders to take us to Flossenbürg, and for so long they had felt themselves constricted by the sense of an authority guiding them. When Flossenbürg refused to receive us they were apparently sent off on vague instructions to continue a southward course until they found some place where they could deposit us, and so, in a measure, they felt that they shared our lot and like us were just sailing along into the blue with no certain destination.[7]

Sometime that afternoon they stopped in front of a farmhouse. The men took turns outside at the water pump. The farmer's wife came outside, carrying several loaves of rye bread and a jug of milk. Best said that it was "real good rye bread such as none of us had tasted for years."[8] Then they climbed back into the van, which was much roomier now. Several of them were able to take a nap.

As the daylight began to fade, they found themselves approaching the town of Regensburg. The van wandered around in the city, stopping again and again as the guards tried to find a place for their passengers to spend the night. Time and again they failed.

After dark they ended up at the main entrance to the state prison. This time the guards told everyone to get out. When they climbed the stairs into the building, one of the state prison guards began ordering them about rudely. One of their own guards interrupted him, explaining that they were not ordinary prisoners, but special prisoners who must be treated with courtesy. "Oh!" said a Regensburg guard. "More aristocrats! Well, put them with the other lot on the second floor."⁹ As it was everywhere, things were very tight. The men slept five to a cell, with three straw mattresses covering the cell floor.

In the morning the cell doors were opened, and the men were allowed to go down the hall to the lavatory. But what a sight they saw: crowding the entire hall were men, women, and children, all family members of the men who had been involved in the Stauffenberg plot—the bombing of Hitler's Wolf's Lair that had gone wrong in June. In fact, a number of Stauffenberg's family members were there.

Best found himself being introduced to so many people that it seemed more like a festive party than a line to use the bathroom in a prison. It was as if the inmates had taken control of the prison. They continued talking with each other and would not return to their cells. Eventually the guards managed to lure them back with breakfast.

POLITICAL PRISONERS

Political prisoners were German citizens who were arrested for speaking out against the Nazis or for offending them in some way. Many of them were considered "Aryan" and were high-ranking people in German society. They were made to wear a red triangle on their clothes, while the Jews wore a yellow star. These people were generally treated better than the other prisoners, but many of them suffered the same sad fate in the end.

Around five that afternoon, one of the guards who had driven the van from Buchenwald declared it was time to leave. The fourteen Buchenwald prisoners gathered their things, said their good-byes, and went down to their van again. Everyone's spirits were very much improved as they headed out again.

But they were only a few miles outside of town when the van violently lurched—and stopped dead. The steering was broken, and it couldn't be repaired. When a lonely bicycle approached them, the guards stopped the rider and asked that he inform the police in Regensburg, so they could send another van. The bicyclist said he would and pedaled off. Darkness fell, and it got cold. Hours passed, but no one ever came. Finally dawn arrived. At last a motorcycle appeared. The guards wouldn't take any chances, so one of them rode on the back of it into Regensburg. It was the morning of April 6, the Friday after Easter.

Help arrived at eleven o'clock, in the form of a huge bus with large plate-glass windows and comfortable seats. The bus came with its own crew of about ten machine-gun-toting military police. The three Buchenwald guards stayed behind with the broken-down heap of a van.

In the early afternoon, a bus came to the small village of Schönberg and stopped in front of the village school, a squarish white building of four stories. They had reached their destination. As it happened, the large group of aristocrats that they had left behind in Regensburg had already arrived here. So the number of political prisoners was 150.

Bonhoeffer and his fellow prisoners were taken into the school and shown into a large room on the first floor. This was to be their common cell. The room had been a girls' hospital wing and was set up with rows of feather beds with bright blankets. It was all very cheering. Best said that despite the "fatigue and hunger we were all in the highest spirits, nervous, excited, and almost hysterical in our laughter."[10] There were large windows on three sides of the room. Now everyone could look out and drink in the green scenery of the valley. Each person chose his bed.

Bonhoeffer sunned himself at one of the windows, praying and thinking. He spent time talking with the others. And he still had a few books with him to comfort him, including the Bible.

LAUGHTER AS A WEAPON

Laughter can be a weapon, and hope can take root in the unlikeliest places. Concentration camp prisoners often fought to keep humor, beauty, and the human spirit alive, even as the Nazis tried to beat them down. One inmate said that "Heroism was in the will to create, to paint, to write, to perform and to compose" in the worst places on earth. Some prisoners snuck in instruments and played music. Some put on plays. Some drew and painted. Others used humor and jokes. Hitler was terribly afraid of being laughed at, and he made jokes such as these a crime:

- There are two kinds of Aryans: non-Aryans and barb-Aryans.
- If Hitler, Göring, and Goebbels were on a ship in a storm and the ship would sink, who would be saved? Answer: Germany.

- Several SS storm troopers enter a church during a Sunday morning service. "My fellow Germans," begins their leader. "I am ordering all those here whose fathers are Jews to leave this church at once." Several worshipers get up and leave. "And now I am ordering out all those whose mothers are Jewish." At this, the pastor jumps up, picks up the statue of Jesus, and says, "Brother, now it's time for you and me to get out."[11]

After they settled in, they became aware of their hunger and banged on the door of their room till a guard arrived. There was no food to be had in the town. The closest food was twenty-five miles away, and for such a trip they would need gasoline, which they did not have. There was nothing to do but go to sleep.

When the prisoners awoke the following day, there was still no breakfast. At some point, a kind soul from the village heard of the "special prisoners" and their troubles. Potato salad and two large loaves of bread were sent over. This was all the food they would have that day, and it was likely the last food Bonhoeffer ever ate. It was Saturday, April 7.

Hugh Falconer, a British officer and fellow prisoner, wrote later to Bonhoeffer's brother-in-law, Gerhard Leibholz: "[Bonhoeffer] was very happy during the whole the time I knew him, and did a great deal to keep some of the weaker [men] from depression and anxiety."[12]

BONHOEFFER'S LAST DAY

The next day, April 8, was the first Sunday after Easter. Bonhoeffer was asked to hold a service for the prisoners. This would be the last time that Dietrich performed the duties of a pastor. He prayed and read the verses for that day. One verse was Isaiah 53:5—"With his stripes we are healed"(rsv). Another was 1 Peter 1:3—"Blessed be the God and Father of our Lord Jesus Christ! By his great mercy we have been born anew to a living hope through the resurrection of Jesus Christ from the dead" (rsv). He then explained these verses to everyone. Captain Best described the service:

> [He] spoke to us in a manner which reached the hearts of all, finding just the right words to express the spirit of our imprisonment and the thoughts and resolutions which it had brought. . . .
>
> He had hardly finished his last prayer when the door opened and two evil-looking men in civilian clothes came in and said:
>
> "Prisoner Bonhoeffer. Get ready to come with us." Those words "Come with us"—for all prisoners they had come to mean one thing only—[execution].
>
> We bade him good-bye—he drew me aside—"This is the end," he said. "For me the beginning of life." [13]

THE BEGINNING OF LIFE

For Dietrich Bonhoeffer, death wasn't something to be feared—he knew heaven would come right after. He knew he was going to be with God.

Bonhoeffer talked about death and fear in many of his sermons. But more importantly, his actions matched what he preached. In a sermon he preached while a pastor in London, he said:

> [L]ife only really begins when it ends here on earth. [A]ll that is here is only the prologue before the curtain goes up—that is for young and old alike to think about. Why are we so afraid when we think about death? . . . Death is only dreadful for those who live in dread and fear of it. [14]

Bonhoeffer asked Captain Best to send his regards to his friend in England, Bishop George Bell. Six years later, in a letter to the Bonhoeffer family, Best recalled what he had written about Bonhoeffer in his book: he "was a good and saintly man." But in the letter he went further: "In fact my feeling was far stronger than these words imply. He was, without exception, the finest and most lovable man I have ever met." [15]

Bonhoeffer was on his way back to the Flossenbürg concentration camp. The journey that Sunday afternoon was one of about a hundred miles. He had a book of poetry with him to read on the way.

Bonhoeffer's sentence of death was almost certainly ordered by Hitler himself. Even Hitler must have known that the war was lost for him and for Germany at that point. But he would do anything for revenge.

Bonhoeffer arrived at Flossenbürg sometime late on Sunday. The camp doctor there gave the following account of Bonhoeffer's last minutes alive:

> On the morning of that day between five and six o'clock the prisoners . . . were taken from their cells, and the verdicts of the court martial read out to them. Through the half-open door in one room of the huts I saw Pastor Bonhoeffer, before taking off his prison [clothes], kneeling on the floor praying fervently to his God. I was most deeply moved by the way this lovable man prayed, so devout and so certain that God heard his prayer. At the place of execution, he again said a short prayer and then climbed the steps to the gallows, brave and composed. His death ensued after a few seconds. In the almost fifty years that I worked as a doctor, I have hardly ever seen a man die so entirely submissive to the will of God.[16]

THINK ABOUT IT

1. Why wasn't Bonhoeffer afraid to die?
2. Bonhoeffer's last sermon was on the resurrection of Jesus. Why would that story give hope to people who might soon die?
3. Time and time again, people remembered how Bonhoeffer encouraged others. Write down at least three different ways you can encourage those around you.

4. All the time Bonhoeffer was in prison, he read, wrote, prayed, had deep talks with people, and even tried to learn some Russian. How might keeping your mind active help you get through tough times?

5. People knew Bonhoeffer was a Christian by the way he spoke and acted. How should you speak and act so that people will know you are a Christian too?

CHAPTER 16

THE MARTYR

1945

Two weeks later, on April 23, the Allies marched into the Flossenbürg concentration camp and freed the prisoners. Within another week Hitler had taken his own life—too cowardly to face defeat and the punishment for his crimes against the world. The war was over. At that point neither Maria nor anyone in Dietrich's family knew what had become of him. His sister Sabine did not hear about her twin brother's death until May 31:

Pastor [**Julius**] **Rieger** telephoned to us from London and asked whether we were home because he had something to say to us. [Gerhard]'s reply on the telephone was "We would be very glad to see you."

Soon from the window I saw our friend arriving at the house. The moment I opened the door to him I felt fear. The expression of his face was so pale and drawn that I knew that something serious had happened. We quickly entered the room where [Gerhard] was, and then Pastor Rieger said with deep sadness, "It's Dietrich. He is no more—and Klaus too."[1]

That July, Karl and Paula Bonhoeffer wrote to Sabine and Gerhard. Before that, communication between Berlin and the outside world had been nearly impossible. They had heard Dietrich had been killed, but had not had any official word of it yet.

23rd July 1945

My dearest children,

We have just been told that an opportunity has arisen for us to send you our greetings and news. It is now three years, I believe, since we received the last letters from you. Now we have just heard that [Gerhard] sent a telegram to Switzerland in order to obtain news of the fate of our dear Dietrich. From this we conclude that you are all still alive, and that is a great consolation for us in our deep sorrow over the fate of our dear Klaus, Dietrich and Rüdiger.

Dietrich spent eighteen months in the military prison at Tegel. Last October he was handed over to the Gestapo and transferred to the SS prison . . . During the early days of February he was taken from there to various concentration camps such as Buchenwald and Flossenbürg . . . We did not know where he was.

His fiancée, Maria von Wedemeyer, who was living with us at this time, attempted to find out for herself where he was. But in this she was unsuccessful. After the victory of the Allies we heard that Dietrich was still alive. But later we received news that he had been murdered by the Gestapo a little before the Americans arrived.[2]

Meanwhile a memorial service was organized for Dietrich and Klaus Bonhoeffer. Dietrich's sister Sabine and her husband

Gerhard, Pastors Rieger and Hildebrandt, and the English Bishop Bell put everything together. It was to be held on July 27 at Holy Trinity Brompton Church, London. Bishop Bell had asked permission to broadcast it in Germany as well, and they agreed.

It was that memorial service at the Holy Trinity Brompton Church the Bonhoeffer parents listened to in their home. The service began with the familiar English hymn, "For All the Saints," and then Bishop Bell prayed. Another hymn, "Hark, a Herald Voice Is Calling," was sung in both English and German. Then the gospel lesson was read. Appropriately enough, it was from the Sermon on the Mount.

FOR ALL THE SAINTS

For all the saints, who from their labors rest,
who thee by faith before the world confessed,
thy name, O Jesus, be forever blest.
Alleluia, Alleluia!

O may thy soldiers, faithful, true, and bold,
fight as the saints who nobly fought of old,
and win with them the victor's crown of gold.
Alleluia, Alleluia!

And when the strife is fierce, the warfare long,
steals on the ear the distant triumph song,
and hearts are brave again, and arms are strong.
Alleluia, Alleluia!

> From earth's wide bounds, from ocean's farthest coast,
> through gates of pearl streams in the countless host,
> singing to Father, Son, and Holy Ghost:
> Alleluia, Alleluia!

After that Bishop Bell preached:

[Dietrich] was quite clear in his convictions, and for all that he was so young and unassuming, he saw the truth and spoke it out with absolute freedom and without fear. When he came to me all unexpectedly in 1942 at Stockholm as the emissary of the Resistance to Hitler, he was, as always, absolutely open and quite untroubled about his own person, his safety. Wherever he went and whoever he spoke with—whether young or old— he was fearless, regardless of himself and, with it all, devoted his heart and soul to his parents, his friends, his country as God willed it to be, to his Church and to his Master.[3]

Bell ended his sermon with the words, "The blood of martyrs is the seed of the Church." Franz Hildebrandt—one of Dietrich's dearest friends—also gave a sermon and ended with these words:

We know not what to do. After these anxious weeks of uncertainty through which we have lived with you, dear Sabine and [Gerhard], and with your parents, we know less than ever how to carry on without the counsel of our brother on whom we could lean and who was so desperately needed by the Church at this time. Today we understand what [it means to say]: "with him a piece of my own life is carried to the grave." Yet: our eyes are upon [God]. We believe in the communion of saints, the forgiveness of sins, the resurrection of the body and the life everlasting. We give thanks to God for the life, the suffering, the witness of our brother whose friends we were privileged to be. We pray God to lead us, too, through his discipleship from this world into His heavenly kingdom; to fulfil in us that other word with which Dietrich concluded . . . "while in God confiding I cannot but rejoice."[4]

When the service ended, Karl and Paula Bonhoeffer turned off the radio.

LIST OF KEY WORDS
AND PEOPLE

Allies: Allied powers during WWII fought against the Nazi
regime. They were Great Britain, France (except during
1940–1944), the Soviet Union (Russia), the United States,
and China. Other members included Australia, Belgium,
Canada, Costa Rica, Cuba, Czechoslovakia, Dominican
Republic, Greece, Guatemala, Haiti, Honduras, India,
Luxembourg, the Netherlands, New Zealand, Nicaragua,
Norway, Panama, Poland, Salvador, South Africa,
Yugoslavia, the Philippines, Mexico, Ethiopia, Iraq, Free
French, and Free Danes.

anti-Semitism: hatred of the Jewish people. *See page 64.*

Aryan Paragraph: law forbidding the inclusion of non-
Aryan people in various government organizations

Aryan: in Nazi Germany, generally referred to a person of
native German ancestry, without any traceable bloodline
from "inferior" groups of people. The typical ideal Aryan
was blond haired and blue eyed.

assassinate: to kill a prominent person by surprise or
secret attack

Axis: Axis powers in World War II were Germany, Italy, and Japan. These countries fought with Hitler in the war.

Barmen Declaration: 1934 statement of the Confessing Church, outlining their values. Released to oppose the Reichskirche, or Nazi church.

Barth, Karl: Swiss theologian; professor, mentor, friend of Dietrich Bonhoeffer

BBC radio: radio station of the British Broadcasting Company, broadcasting news and culture programs all over Europe and the world

Beck, General Ludwig: German general who resigned quietly in protest of Hitler's policies

Bell, George: bishop in the Church of England, friend of Dietrich Bonhoeffer

Bethge, Eberhard: close friend of Dietrich Bonhoeffer, pastor, and student at illegal seminary

Bonhoeffer, Christine: older sister of Dietrich Bonhoeffer. Wife of Hans von Dohnanyi.

Bonhoeffer, Dietrich: pastor, theologian, and resistance member. Youngest son of Karl and Paula Bonhoeffer.

Bonhoeffer, Karl-Friedrich: oldest son of Karl and Paula Bonhoeffer, older brother of Dietrich Bonhoeffer

Bonhoeffer, Karl: world-famous German psychiatrist and neurologist. Father of Dietrich Bonhoeffer.

Bonhoeffer, Klaus: third son of Paula and Karl Bonhoeffer. Older brother of Deitrich Bonhoeffer. Executed by Nazis for participating in the German resistance.

Bonhoeffer, Sabine: twin sister of Dietrich Bonhoeffer. Married Gerhard Leibholz.

Bonhoeffer, Susanne: youngest daughter of Karl and Paula Bonhoeffer, Dietrich Bonhoeffer's younger sister

Bonhoeffer, Ursula: oldest daughter of Karl and Paula Bonhoeffer, older sister of Dietrich Bonhoeffer. Married to Rudiger Schleicher, who was executed for being a member of the German resistance.

Bonhoeffer, Walter: second son of Karl and Paula Bonhoeffer. Older brother of Dietrich Bonhoeffer. Killed at age nineteen while fighting in World War I.

boycott: form of protest in which people refuse to deal with certain people or organizations

Canaris, Admiral Wilhelm: anti-Hitler head of German Military Intelligence, secret leader in the German resistance, Dohnanyi's boss, responsible for the Chronicle of Shame

Chamberlain, Neville: British prime minister at the beginning of World War II, from 1937 to 1940. Responsible for the Munich Agreement with Hitler.

Chronicle of Shame: aka Zossen File, collection of evidence of Nazi atrocities collected by Hans von Dohnanyi and Wilhelm Canaris

Churchill, Winston: British Prime Minister during World War II, from May 10, 1940, onward. Before that, he was a war minister with the British Government.

Communists: a political party (the German Communist Party) who rivaled the Nazis after World War I

concentration camps: in Nazi territories, camps where Jews, political prisoners, and "undesirables" were detained. Known for shocking conditions and near-certain death. See *death camps.*

Confessing Church: Christian church denomination founded by Dietrich Bonhoeffer and others who opposed the Nazi church

conspiracy: organized effort to secretly overthrow or do another unlawful act. *See page 142.*

coup d'état: a sudden overthrowing of a government by a small group. *See page 88.*

death camps: in Nazi territories, camps where Jews, political prisoners, and "undesirables" were sent to be killed. Death camps used gassing, firing squads, hanging, and other forms of murder.

enlist: to sign up to fight in a military force

evangelist: a person who tells others about one's faith

fanatic: someone who is overly excited about or devoted to something. *See page 78.*

Ferdinand, Franz: Archduke of Austro-Hungary, whose assassination set off events that would lead to World War I

Fisher, Albert Franklin "Frank": African-American student at Union Theological Seminary in New York. Friend of Dietrich Bonhoeffer.

Führer: German word for "leader," title given to Adolf Hitler

German Christians: name given to members of the Nazi Christian church during Hitler's reign. Not all Christians in Germany were considered "German Christians."

German resistance: secret, underground organization of Germans who plotted to bring down Hitler and the Nazis from within Germany

Gestapo: Nazi police force in charge of interrogating and capturing those who opposed the Nazi party

Goebbels, Joseph: Nazi minister of propaganda

Great Depression: worldwide economic disaster that lasted from 1929 until the early 1940s

Hildebrandt, Franz: close friend of Dietrich Bonhoeffer. Fellow Christian pastor, who had to flee from Nazi Germany because of Jewish ancestry.

Himmler, Heinrich: Nazi head of the SS military police

Hitler, Adolf: German chancellor during World War II, despotic ruler responsible for the Holocaust and aggressions of World War II

Holocaust: the time period in which millions of European civilians and especially Jews were killed by the Nazis during World War II

infantry: a branch of an army made up of soldiers trained, armed, and equipped to fight on foot

interrogate: formal questioning of prisoner, usually through forceful means. *See page 191.*

Jazz Age: period of economic prosperity and freewheeling growth in the 1920s, particularly in America. Ended in the Great Depression.

Judaism: the faith of the Jews. The story of the Jews and God is told in the Old Testament of the Bible.

kaiser: German word for "emperor"

Leibholz, Gerhard: law professor, married to Sabine Bonhoeffer. Left Germany during WWII due to Jewish heritage. Brother-in-law of Deitrich Bonhoeffer.

Leiper, Henry: lecturer at Union Theological Seminary. Dietrich Bonhoeffer's supervisor during his second trip to America in 1939.

Luftwaffe: German air force

Luther, Martin: German priest who started the Protestant Reformation in 1517—a splitting from the Catholic Church that formed Protestant churches

Lutheran: a division of Protestant Christianity named after its founder, Martin Luther. Many German Protestants are traditionally Lutheran.

manifesto: a piece of writing that publically declares and explains one's views. *See page 25.*

mark: German form of money

martyr: a person who is killed or who suffers greatly for a religion or cause. *See page 6.*

Müller, Joseph: German lawyer, member of the German resistance

Müller, Ludwig: Hitler's choice for bishop of the Nazi church, the Reichskirche

Munich Agreement: agreement made by British Prime Minister Neville Chamberlain and Hitler in 1938, designed to give Hitler parts of the *Sudetenland* (Czechoslovakia), if he promised to invade no further. Broken at the start of World War II.

muzzling decree: a law designed to stop free speech

Nazis: members of the political party of Hitler, also known as the Third Reich

neo-orthodoxy: modern practice of traditional or "orthodox" theology

neurology: the scientific study of the brain and nervous system

newsreel: a short movie containing news and current events. *See page 3.*

Niemöller, Martin: leader in the church struggle against Hitler. Founder of the Pastors Emergency League. Imprisoned in a concentration camp during WWII.

Nuremberg Laws: "Laws for the Protection of German Blood and German Honor," designed to exclude Jews from parts of everyday German life.

pacifism: opposition to war or violence as a means of settling disputes. *See page 94.*

parliament: the highest law-making group of certain types of government

pastor: a minister or priest in charge of a church or parish. *See page 6.*

propaganda: organized spreading of ideas, typically through media. *See page 58.*

prophet: a spokesperson of some doctrine, cause, or movement. *See page 6.*

psychiatry: a branch of medicine that deals with disorders of the mind, emotions, or behavior

Reformation: religious protests against the Catholic church, started by Martin Luther in Germany in the 1500s. Led to the founding of Protestant churches.

Reichskirche: the Nazi-approved German Christian church

Rieger, Julius: German pastor based in London, friend of Dietrich Bonhoeffer

Roeder, Manfred: Dietrich Bonhoeffer's prosecutor at Tegel prison

seminary: a training school for pastors or other clergy

SS: branch of elite Nazi police

spy: a person who tries secretly to get information about a country or organization for another country or organization. *See page 6.*

subversive: undermining or overthrowing. *See page 148.*

Sudetenland: German-speaking part of Czechoslovakia

swastika: symbol of the Nazi party, a cross with bent arms

T-4 euthanasia program: program of the Nazi government in which German children with genetic defects, along with other "incurables," were killed.

Tegel military prison: German prison where Dietrich Bonhoeffer was kept from April 1943 to October 1944

theology: the study of religion

Third Reich: the Nazi government, or "Third Kingdom"

Traub, Hellmut: pastor who took over for Dietrich in the illegal seminaries while he was in America

Treaty of Versailles: treaty ending World War I, penalizing Germany

Valkyrie: failed June 1943 plot to kill Hitler. Also, a Norse mythological figure.

von Dohnanyi, Hans: German lawyer, leader in the German resistance, keeper of the Chronicle of Shame. Married to Christine Bonhoeffer, brother-in-law of Dietrich Bonhoeffer.

von Kleist-Retzow, Ruth: grandmother of Maria von Wedemeyer

von Hase, Paul: uncle of Dietrich Bonhoeffer. General in the Nazi German Army, leader in the German resistance, military commandant of Berlin (and therefore in charge of Tegel prison). Uncle of Dietrich Bonhoeffer.

von Hase, Paula: mother of Dietrich Bonhoeffer

von Hindenburg, Paul: president of Germany during
World War II

von Stauffenberg, Colonel Claus: German resistance
leader in charge of the Valkyrie plot

von Wedemeyer, Maria: fiancée of Dietrich Bonhoeffer

Wolfsschanze ("Wolf's Lair"): one of Hitler's secret
headquarters in rural Germany

NOTES

FAMILY TREE

Dietrich Bonhoeffer, *Résistance et soumission: Lettres et notes de captivité* (Geneva: Editions Labor et Fides, 2006), 558.

Geneall.com, "Karl Friedrich Bonhoeffer," accessed October 30, 2014, http://geneall.net/de/name/2104119/karl-friedrich-bonhoeffer/.

Ferdinand Schlingensiepen, *Dietrich Bonhoeffer 1906-1945: Martyr, Thinker, Man of Resistance* (New York: T&T Clark International, 2010), 430.

Chemeurope.com, "Karl Friedrich Bonhoeffer," accessed October 30, 2014, http://chemeurope.com/en/encyclopedia/Karl_Friedrich_Bonhoeffer.html.

Dietrich Bonhoeffer, *Dietrich Bonhoeffer Works, Volume II: Ecumenical, Academic, and Pastoral Work, 1931-1932* (Minneapolis, MN: Augsburg Fortress, 2012), 580.

CHAPTER 1: THE END

1. *Encyclopædia Britannica Online*, s.v. "Allied Powers," accessed October 08, 2014, http://www.britannica.com/EBchecked/topic/16380/Allied-Powers; *Encyclopædia Britannica Online*, s.v. "Axis Powers," accessed October 08, 2014, http://www.britannica.com/EBchecked/topic/46315/Axis-Powers.

2. By permission. From *Merriam-Webster's Learners® Dictionary* © 2015 by Merriam-Webster, Inc. (http://www.learnersdictionary.com).

3. By permission. From *Merriam-Webster's Learners® Dictionary* © 2015 by Merriam-Webster, Inc. (http://www.learnersdictionary.com); *Random House Webster's Unabridged Dictionary*, s.v. "prophet," 2nd ed. New York: Random House, 2001; By permission. From *Merriam-Webster's Learners® Dictionary* © 2015 by Merriam-Webster, Inc. (http://www.learnersdictionary.com); Ibid.

CHAPTER 2: A MISCHIEVOUS BOY AND THE GREAT WAR

1. Eberhard Bethge, *Dietrich Bonhoeffer: A Biography*, rev. ed. (Minneapolis: Augsburg Fortress, 2000), 8.
2. Sabine Leibholz-Bonhoeffer, *The Bonhoeffers: Portrait of a Family* (New York, St. Martin's Press, 1971), 37.
3. Mary Bosanquet, *The Life and Death of Dietrich Bonhoeffer* (New York: Harper and Row, 1968), 29.
4. Bethge, *Dietrich Bonhoeffer: A Biography*, 24.
5. Sabine Leibholz-Bonhoeffer, *The Bonhoeffers: Portrait of a Family* (New York, St. Martin's Press, 1971), 4.
6. Bethge, *Dietrich Bonhoeffer: A Biography*, 26.
7. Leibholz-Bonhoeffer, *The Bonhoeffers*, 17.
8. Jonathan Buff, "World War I: Training to Be a Soldier (British Library)," accessed October 13, 2014, http://www.bl.uk/world-war-one/articles/training-to-be-a-soldier; US Department of Justice, "WWI Casualty and Death Tables (NPT)," accessed October 8, 2014, http://www.pbs.org/greatwar/resources/casdeath_pop.html.
9. Leibholz-Bonhoeffer, *The Bonhoeffers*, 22–23.
10. Ibid., 21–22.
11. PBS, "WWI Timeline: 1914," accessed January 9, 2015, http://www.pbs.org/greatwar/timeline/time_1914.html; History on the Net, "World War One Timeline," accessed January 9, 2015, http://www.historyonthenet.com/ww1/ww1_timeline.htm.
12. Wolf-Dieter Zimmermann and Ronald G. Smith, eds., *I Knew Dietrich Bonhoeffer*, trans. Käthe Gregor Smith (New York: Harper and Row, 1966), 31.

CHAPTER 3: OFF TO UNIVERSITY

1. *The Young Bonhoeffer: 1918–1927*, vol. 9, *Dietrich Bonheoffer Works*, trans. and ed. Hans Pfeifer et al. (New York: Fortress Press, 2002), 64.
2. United States Department of Labor, *Retail Prices of Food, 1923–36*, Bulletin No. 635 (Washington, DC: U.S. Government Printing Office, October 1937), http://fraser.stlouisfed.org/docs/publications/bls/193710_bls_635retailpr.pdf.
3. *Random House Webster's Unabridged Dictionary*, s.v. "manifesto." 2nd ed. New York: Random House, 2001.
4. *The Young Bonhoeffer*, 78.
5. Ibid., 83.
6. Ibid., 89.
7. *Letters and Papers from Prison*, vol. 8, *Dietrich Bonhoeffer Works*, ed. John W. Degruchy (Minneapolis: Augsburg Fortress, 2010), 382.
8. *The Young Bonhoeffer*, 111.
9. Karl Barth, *God in Action*, trans. Elmer George Homrighausen and Karl Julius Ernst (New York: Round Table Press, 1936), 39–57; Ibid., 39–57; Karl Barth, *Letters, 1961–1968*, ed. Geoffrey Bromiley (Grand Rapids, MI: Eerdmans, 1981), 284.

CHAPTER 4: VENTURING ABROAD

1. *Barcelona, Berlin, New York: 1928–1931*, vol. 10, *Dietrich Bonhoeffer Works*, ed. Clifford J. Green, trans Douglas W. Stott (New York: Fortress Press, 2008), 60.
2. Ibid., 62.
3. Dietrich Bonhoeffer to Paula Bonhoeffer, Barcelona, February 20, 1928.
4. *Barcelona, Berlin, New York*, 527–31.
5. Ibid., 139.
6. The History Channel, "The Roaring Twenties," accessed October 8, 2014, http://www.history.com/topics/roaring-twenties; Tim Dirks, "AMC Filmsite: The Jazz Singer (1927)," accessed October 8, 2014, http://www.filmsite.org/jazz.html; "The Internet Guide

to Jazz Age Slang," accessed October 8, 2014, http://home.
earthlink.net/~dlarkins/slang-pg.htm.

7. *Barcelona, Berlin, New York: 1928–1931*, 265–66.
8. Ibid., 308.
9. "Big Questions and Answers for Little People," Praise Factory,
accessed February 16, 2015, http://www.praisefactory.org/
curriculum.
10. *Barcelona, Berlin, New York: 1928–1931*, 309–10.
11. Ibid., 309–10.

CHAPTER 5: A NEW WAY OF SEEING THE CHURCH

1. *Barcelona, Berlin, New York: 1928–1931*, vol. 10, *Dietrich
Bonhoeffer Works*, ed. Clifford J. Green, trans. Douglas W. Stott
(New York: Fortress Press, 2008), 293.
2. Eberhard Bethge, *Dietrich Bonhoeffer: A Biography*, rev. ed.
(Minneapolis: Augsburg Fortress, 2000), 151.
3. *Barcelona, Berlin, New York*, 439.
4. Wolf-Dieter Zimmermann and Ronald G. Smith, eds., *I Knew
Dietrich Bonhoeffer*, trans. Käthe Gregor Smith (New York:
Harper and Row, 1966), 60.
5. Ibid., 68.
6. Inge Karding, interview by Martin Doblmeier, *Bonhoeffer:
Pastor, Pacifist, Nazi Resister. A documentary film by Martin
Doblmeier*, Princeton University. Unused footage quoted here by
permission of the director.
7. Zimmermann and Smith, *I Knew Dietrich Bonhoeffer*, 64–65.
8. Inge Karding, interview by Martin Doblmeier.

CHAPTER 6: NAZI LIES

1. Richard Steigman-Gall, *The Holy Reich: Nazi Conceptions of
Christianity, 1919–1945*, (Cambridge: Cambridge University
Press, 2003), 116.

2. Ibid., 116.
3. Eberhard Bethge, *Dietrich Bonhoeffer: A Biography*, rev. ed. (Minneapolis: Augsburg Fortress, 2000), 257.
4. William L. Shirer, *The Rise and Fall of the Third Reich: A History of Nazi Germany* (New York: Simon and Schuster, 1960), 194.
5. *No Rusty Swords: Letters, Lectures and Notees 1928–1936*, vol. 1, *Collected Works of Dietrich Bonhoeffer*, ed. Edwin H. Robertson, trans. Edwin H. Robertson and John Bowden (New York: Harper and Row, 1965), 226.
6. By permission. From *Merriam-Webster's Learners® Dictionary* © 2015 by Merriam-Webster, Inc. (http://www.learnersdictionary.com).
7. Sabine Leibholz-Bonhoeffer, *The Bonhoeffers: Portrait of a Family* (New York: St. Martin's Press, 1971), 84.
8. Elizabeth Raum, *Dietrich Bonhoeffer: Called by God* (New York: Simon and Schuster, 1960), 80.
9. National Public Television, "America and the Holocaust: People & Events: Joseph Goebbels (1897-1945)," 2009, http://www.pbs.org/wgbh/amex/holocaust/peopleevents/pandeAMEX98.html; *Encyclopædia Britannica Online*, s.v. "Joseph Goebbels," 2014, http://www.britannica.com/EBchecked/topic/236986/Joseph-Goebbels.
10. Shirer, *The Rise and Fall of the Third Reich*, 240.
11. *Encyclopædia Britannica Online*, s. v. "Swastika," 2014, http://www.britannica.com/EBchecked/topic/576371/swastika; United States Holocaust Memorial Museum, "Swastika," 2014, http://www.ushmm.org/search/results.php?q=swastika&q__src=&q__grp=&q__typ=&q__mty=&q__sty=&q__lng=&max_page_docs=25&start_doc=1.
12. Doris L. Bergen, *Twisted Cross: The German Christian Movement in the Third Reich* (Chapel Hill, NC: University of North Carolina Press, 1996), 68.

CHAPTER 7: WORSHIPING GOD . . . OR HITLER?

1. William L. Shirer, *The Rise and Fall of the Third Reich: A History of Nazi Germany* (New York: Simon and Schuster, 1960), 238.
2. *Random House Webster's Unabridged Dictionary,* s.v. "fanatic." 2nd ed. New York: Random House, 2001.
3. *Encyclopædia Britannica Online,* s.v. "Hitler Youth," accessed October 04, 2014, http://www.britannica.com/EBchecked/topic/268111/Hitler-Youth.
4. Hermann Rauschning, *The Voice of Destruction* (Gretna, Louisiana: Pelican, 1940), 252.
5. Eberhard Bethge, *Dietrich Bonhoeffer: A Biography,* rev. ed. (Minneapolis: Augsburg Fortress, 2000), 341.
6. James Bentley, *Martin Niemöller: 1892–1984* (New York: Free Press, 1984), 86.
7. *London: 1933–1935,* vol. 13, *Dietrich Bonhoeffer Works,* ed. Keith Clements, trans. Isabel Best (New York: Fortress Press, 2007), 97–98.
8. Ibid., 179–80.
9. By permission. From *Merriam-Webster's Word Central* © 2015 by Merriam-Webster, Inc. (http://www.wordcentral.com).
10. Shirer, *The Rise and Fall of the Third Reich,* 226.
11. Inge Karding, interview by Martin Doblmeier, *Bonhoeffer: Pastor, Pacifist, Nazi Resister. A documentary film by Martin Doblmeier,* Princeton University. Unused footage quoted here by permission of the director.

CHAPTER 8: SECRET SEMINARIES

1. Wolf-Dieter Zimmermann and Ronald G. Smith, eds., *I Knew Dietrich Bonhoeffer,* trans. Käthe Gregor Smith (New York: Harper and Row, 1966), 91.
2. By permission. From *Merriam-Webster's Learners®️ Dictionary* © 2015 by Merriam-Webster, Inc. (http://www.learnersdictionary.com); BBC, "Ethics Guide: Pacifism," accessed October 13, 2014, http://www.bbc.co.uk/ethics/war/against/pacifism_1.shtml.

3. Eberhard Bethge, *Dietrich Bonhoeffer: A Biography*, rev. ed. (Minneapolis, Augsburg Fortress, 2000), 4.

4. *London: 1933–1935*, vol. 13, *Dietrich Bonhoeffer Works*, ed. Keith Clements, trans. Isabel Best (new York: Fortress Press, 2007), 308–09.

5. Inge Karding, interview by Martin Doblmeier, *Bonhoeffer: Pastor, Pacifist, Nazi Resister. A documentary film by Martin Doblmeier*, Princeton University. Unused footage quoted here by permission of the director.

6. Bethge, *Dietrich Bonhoeffer*, 394.

7. Albert Schönherr, interview by Martin Doblmeier, *Bonhoeffer: Paster, Pacifish, Nazi Resister. A documentary film by Martin Doblmeier*, Princeton University. Unused footage quoted here by permission of the director.

8. Germany, *Nuremberg Laws*, September 15, 1935.

9. Bethge, *Dietrich Bonhoeffer*, 512.

10. *The Way to Freedom: Letters, Lectures and Notes, 1935–1939*, vol. 2, *Collected Words of Dietrich Bonhoeffer*, ed. Edwin H. Robertson, trans. Edwin H. Robertson and John Bowden (New York: Harper and Row, 1966), 151.

11. Olympics.org, "Jesse Owens's Inspiring History" (video), 2013, http://www.olympic.org/videos/jesse-owens-s-inspiring-history, accessed October 30, 2014; Jewish Virtual Library, "The Nazi Party: The Nazi Olympics, August 1936," accessed October 13, 2014, http://www.jewishvirtuallibrary.org/jsource/Holocaust/olympics.html; PBS: The American Experience, "Jesse Owens," accessed October 13, 2014, http://www.pbs.org/wgbh/americanexperience/features/introduction/owens/.

12. James Bentley, *Martin Niemöller: 1892–1984* (New York: Free Press, 1984), 129.

13. *Encyclopædia Britannica Online*, s.v. "SS," accessed October 08, 2014, http://www.britannica.com/EBchecked/topic/562059/SS; *Encyclopædia Britannica Online*, s.v. "Gestapo," accessed October 08, 2014, http://www.britannica.com/EBchecked/topic/232117/Gestapo.

14. Bethge, *Dietrich Bonhoeffer*, 591.

CHAPTER 9: RUMBLINGS OF WAR

1. Hans B. Gisevius, *To the Bitter End: An Insider's Account of the Plot to Kill Hitler 1933–1944*, trans. Richard Winston and Clara Winston (New York: Da Capo Press, 1998), 363.

2. William L. Shirer, *The Rise and Fall of the Third Reich: A History of Nazi Germany* (New York: Simon and Schuster, 1960), 317–19.

3. Sabine Leibholz-Bonhoeffer, *The Bonhoeffers: Portrait of a Family* (New York: St. Martin's Press, 1971), 92.

4. Central Intelligence Agency, "Navajo Code Talkers and the Unbreakable Code, 2008, https://www.cia.gov/news-information/featured-story-archive/2008-featured-story-archive/navajo-code-talkers/; US Navy, "Navajo Code Talkers' Dictionary, undated, accessed October 4, 2008, http://www.history.navy.mil/faqs/faq61-4.htm.

5. Leibholz-Bonhoeffer, *The Bonhoeffers*, 97–100.

6. Dietrich Bonhoeffer, *Life Together*, trans. John W. Doberstein (New York: Harper and Row, 1954), 17.

7. Wolf-Dieter Zimmermann and Ronald G. Smith, eds., *I Knew Dietrich Bonhoeffer*, trans. Käthe Gregor Smith (New York: Harper and Row, 1966), 153–54.

8. Eberhard Bethge, *Dietrich Bonhoeffer: A Biography*, rev. ed. (Minneapolis, Augsburg Fortress, 2000), 644.

9. *The Way to Freedom: Letters, Lectures and Notes 1935–1939*, vol. 2, *Collected Works of Dietrich Bonhoeffer*, ed. Edwin H. Robertson, trans. Edwin H. Robertson and John Bowden (New York: Harper and Row, 1966), 222.

10. Bloomberg Business Week, "Inventions from the Great Depression," 2014, http://images.businessweek.com/ss/08/12/1205_sb_necessity/9.htm.

CHAPTER 10: THE GREAT DECISION

1. *The Way to Freedom: Letters, Lectures and Notes 1935–1939*, vol. 2, *Collected Works of Dietrich Bonhoeffer*, ed. Edwin H. Robertson, trans. Edwin H. Robertson and John Bowden (New York: Harper and Row, 1966), 228–29.

2. Ibid., 228.

3. Dietrich Bonhoeffer, *A Testament to Freedom: The Essential Writings of Dietrich Bonhoeffer*, rev. ed., eds. Geffrey B. Kelly and F. Burton Nelson (New York: Harper One, 1995), 477–78.

4. *The Way to Freedom*, 233.

5. Wolf-Dieter Zimmermann and Ronald G. Smith, eds., *I Knew Dietrich Bonhoeffer*, trans. Käthe Gregor Smith (New York: Harper and Row, 1966), 93.

6. Mary Bosanquet, *The Life and Death of Dietrich Bonhoeffer* (New York: Harper and Row, 1968), 217–18.

7. Zimmermann and Smith, *I Knew Dietrich Bonhoeffer*, 158–60.

8. George Victor, *Hitler: The Pathology of Evil* (Dulles, VA: Brassey's, 1998), 184.

9. "Recognizing Propaganda Techniques and Errors of Faulty Logic," Cuesta College (last updated June 3, 2011), https://academic.cuesta.edu/acasupp/as/404.htm.

10. William L. Shirer, *The Rise and Fall of the Third Reich: A History of Nazi Germany* (New York: Simon and Schuster, 1960), 596.

11. Ibid.

CHAPTER 11: FROM PASTOR TO SPY

1. By permission. From *Merriam-Webster's Learners® Dictionary* © 2015 by Merriam-Webster, Inc. (http://www.learnersdictionary.com).

2. Eberhard Bethge, *Friendship and Resistance: Essays on Dietrich Bonhoeffer* (Grand Rapids, Eerdmans, 1995), 24.

3. Eberhard Bethge, *Dietrich Bonhoeffer: A Biography*, rev. ed. (Minneapolis, Augsburg Fortress, 2000), 681.

4. Joachim Fest, *Plotting Hitler's Death: The German Resistance to Hitler, 1933–1945*, trans. Bruce Little (New York: Metropolitan Books, 1996), 138.

5. By permission. From *Merriam-Webster's Learners® Dictionary* © 2015 by Merriam-Webster, Inc. (http://www.learnersdictionary.com).

6. History on the Net, "World War Two: The Geneva Convention," 2014, http://www.historyonthenet.com/ww2/geneva_convention.htm; Maria Trombly, "Reference Guide to the Geneva Conventions, Convention III, Relative to the Treatment of Prisoners of War, Geneva, 12 August 1949," Society of Professional Journalists, 2003, accessed October 4, http://www.spj.org/gc-text3.asp; ICRC, "Convention relative to the Treatment of Prisoners of War. Geneva, 27 July 1929," (2014), https://www.icrc.org/applic/ihl/ihl.nsf/Treaty.xsp?action=open Document&documentId=0BDEDDD046FDEBA9C12563CD002 D69B1.

7. *Conspiracy and Imprisonment: 1940–1945*, vol. 16, *Dietrich Bonhoeffer Works*, ed. Mark S. Brocker, trans. Lisa E. Dahill with Douglas W. Stott (New York: Fortress Press, 2006), 207–08.

8. Bethge, *Dietrich Bonhoeffer*, 704.

9. Hans B. Gisevius, *To the Bitter End: An Insider's Account of the Plot to Kill Hitler 1933–1944*, trans. Richard Winston and Clara Winston (New York: Da Capo Press, 1998), 435.

CHAPTER 12: MEETING MARIA

1. Ruth-Alice von Bismarck and Ulrich Kabitz, eds., *Love Letters from Cell 92: The Correspondence Between Dietrich Bonhoeffer and Maria von Wedemeyer, 1943–1945*, trans. John Brownjohn (New York: Abingdon Press, 1995), 330.

2. *Conspiracy and Imprisonment: 1940–1945*, vol. 16, *Dietrich Bonhoeffer Works*, ed. Mark S. Brocker, trans. Lisa E. Dahill with Douglas W. Stott (New York: Fortress Press, 2006), 329–30.

3. Ibid., 331.

4. Bob Burns, "Half brother of Hitler runs Berlin restaurant," *The Spartanburg Herald* (1938, January 10): pp. 5, accessed October 4, 2014, http://news.google.com/newspapers?nid=187 6&dat=19380110&id=7S8sAAAAIBAJ&sjid=1MoEAAAAIBAJ &pg=5007,802342.

5. *Conspiracy and Imprisonment*, 366–67.

6. Ibid., 370–71.

7. Ibid., 373–74.
8. Ibid., 374–75.
9. Ethan Trex, "9 Strange Courtship Rituals from Around the World," Mental Floss, October 7, 2011, accessed October 4, 2014, http://mentalfloss.com/ article/28950/9-strange-courtship-rituals-around-world.
10. Bismarck and Kabitz, eds., *Love Letters from Cell 92*, 336.
11. Ibid., 338–39.
12. *Conspiracy and Imprisonment*, 383–84.

CHAPTER 13: CELL 92

1. Wolf-Dieter Zimmermann and Ronald G. Smith, eds. *I Knew Dietrich Bonhoeffer*, trans. Käthe Gregor Smith (New York: Harper and Row, 1966), 190–92.
2. National Geographic Channel, "42 Ways to Kill Hitler, 2014, http://natgeotv.com.au/tv/42-ways-to-kill-hitler/; History.com, "This Day in History, World War II, March 21, 1943: Another Plot to Kill Hitler Foiled," 2014, http://www.history.com/ this-day-in-history/another-plot-to-kill-hitler-foiled.
3. Ruth-Alice von Bismarck and Ulrich Kabitz, eds., *Love Letters from Cell 92: The Correspondence Between Dietrich Bonhoeffer and Maria Von Wedemeyer, 1943–1945*, trans. John Brownjohn (New York: Abingdon Press, 1995), 347.
4. Mary Bosanquet, *The Life and Death of Dietrich Bonhoeffer* (New York: Harper and Row, 1968), 247–48.
5. Eberhard Bethge, *Dietrich Bonhoeffer: A Biography*, rev. ed. (Minneapolis: Augsburg Fortress, 2000), 734.
6. Zimmermann and Smith, *I Knew Dietrich Bonhoeffer*, 222.
7. *Letters and Papers from Prison*, vol. 8, *Dietrich Bonhoeffer Works*, ed. John W. Degruchy (Minneapolis: Augsburg Fortress, 2010), 21–22.
8. Christopher von Dohnanyi, interview by Martin Doblmeier, *Bonhoeffer: Pastor, Pacifist, Nazi Resister. A documentary film by Martin Doblmeier*, Princeton University. Unused footage quoted here by permission of the director.

9. Kate Connolly, "I'm no hero, says woman who saved 2,500 ghetto children," The Guardian, March 14, 2007, http://www.theguardian.com/world/2007/mar/15/secondworldwar.poland; "Dead at 98: Heroic Irena Sendler, who helped save 2,500 Jewish children from the Nazis," Mail Online, May 12, 2008, http://www.dailymail.co.uk/news/article-565969/Dead-98-Heroic-Irena-Sendler-helped-save-2-500-Jewish-children-Nazis.html.
10. Bethge, Dietrich Bonhoeffer, 813–14.
11. Letters and Papers from Prison, 163.
12. Dietrich Bonhoeffer, Ethics (New York: Touchstone, 1995), 19.
13. Bismarck and Kabitz, eds. Love Letters from Cell 92: The Correspondence Between Dietrich Bonhoeffer and Maria von Wedemeyer, 1943–1945, trans. John Brownjohn (New York: Abingdon Press, 1995), 26–27.
14. Ibid., 27.
15. Letters and Papers from Prison, 144–45.

Answer to code throughout entire book, from front to back:

"Action springs not from thought, but from a readiness for responsibility."

For more information about the code, see pages 174–175.

CHAPTER 14: THE CONSPIRACY FAILS

1. Letters and Papers from Prison, vol. 8, Dietrich Bonhoeffer Works, ed. John W. Degruchy (Minneapolis: Augsburg Fortress, 2010), 340–421.
2. Encyclopædia Britannica Online, s.v. "Valkyrie," accessed October 13, 2014, http://www.britannica.com/EBchecked/topic/622196/Valkyrie; Florida Center for Instructional Technology, "A Teacher's Guide to the Holocaust: Nazi Approved Music," (2013), http://fcit.usf.edu/holocaust/arts/musreich.htm.
3. Alex Last, "The German Officer who Tried to Kill Hitler," BBC World Service, July 19, 2014, http://www.bbc.com/news/magazine-28330605.

4. Pierre Galante and Eugene Silianoff, *Operation Valkyrie: The German Generals' Plot Against Hitler* (New York: Harper and Row, 1981), 15.

5. William L. Shirer, *The Rise and Fall of the Third Reich: A History of Nazi Germany* (New York: Simon and Schuster, 1960), 1069.

6. Joachim Fest, *Plotting Hitler's Death: The German Resistance to Hitler, 1933–1945*, trans. Bruce Little (New York: Metropolitan Books, 1996), 278.

7. Ibid., 289–90.

8. By permission. From *Merriam-Webster's Learners® Dictionary* © 2015 by Merriam-Webster, Inc. (http://www.learnersdictionary.com).

9. *Letters and Papers from Prison*, 393–94.

10. PBS, "Timeline of World War II, September 2007, http://www.pbs.org/thewar/at_war_timeline_1944.htm; History Learning Site, "World War Two, 1944," (2014), http://www.historylearningsite.co.uk/1944_world_war_two.htm.

11. Bismarck and Kabitz, *Love Letters from Cell 92*, 268–70.

CHAPTER 15: ON THE ROAD TO FREEDOM

1. Wolf-Dieter Zimmermann and Ronald G. Smith, eds., *I Knew Dietrich Bonhoeffer*, trans. Käthe Gregor Smith (New York: Harper and Row, 1966), 226–30.

2. United States Holocaust Memorial Museum, "Holocaust Encyclopedia: Killing Centers," 2014, http://www.ushmm.org/wlc/en/article.php?ModuleId=10007327; United States Holocaust Memorial Museum, "Holocaust Encyclopedia: Buchenwald," 2014, http://www.ushmm.org/wlc/en/article.php?ModuleId=10005198.

3. Jewish Cultural Centre, "The Holocaust Explained: What Was the Final Solution?" 2011, http://www.theholocaustexplained.org/ks3/the-final solution/#.VCU0hEuZI_s; *Encyclopædia Britannica Online*, s.v. "Holocaust," accessed October 08, 2014, http://www.britannica.com/EBchecked/topic/269548/Holocaust.

4. S. Payne Best, *The Venlo Incident* (Watford, Herts: Hutchinson, 1950), 180.

5. Ibid., 190; Jewish Virtual Library, "Gassing Victims in the Holocaust," accessed January 9, 2015, http://www.jewishvirtuallibrary.org/jsource/Holocaust/gascamp.html.

6. Best, *The Venlo Incident*, 192.

7. Ibid.

8. Ibid., 192–93.

9. Ibid.

10. Ibid., 196.

11. John Morreall, "Humor in the Holocaust: Its Critical, Cohesive, and Coping Functions," Holocaust Teacher Resource Center, November 22, 2001, http://www.holocaust-trc.org/humor-in-the-holocaust/; Curt Daniel, "Theatre in the German Concentration Camps," Theatre Arts, November 1941, http://www.theatrehistory.com/german/holocaust001.html.

12. Sabine Leibholz-Bonhoeffer, *The Bonhoeffers: Portrait of a Family* (New York: St. Martin's Press, 1971), 198–99.

13. Best, *The Venlo Incident*, 192.

14. *London: 1933–1935*, vol. 13, *Dietrich Bonhoeffer Works*, ed. Keith Clements, trans. Isabel Best (New York: Fortress Press, 2007), 331.

15. Eberhard Bethge, *Dietrich Bonhoeffer: A Biography*, rev. ed. (Minneapolis: Augsburg Fortress, 2000), 920.

16. Ibid, 927–28.

CHAPTER 16: THE MARTYR

1. Sabine Leibholz-Bonhoeffer, *The Bonhoeffers: Portrait of a Family* (New York: St. Martin's Press, 1971), 184–86.

2. Ibid., 190.

3. Ibid., 188–89.

4. Amos Cresswell and Maxwell Tow, *Dr. Franz Hildebrandt: Mr. Valiant for Truth* (Grand Rapids: Smyth and Helwys, 2000), 223–27.

ABOUT THE AUTHOR

Eric Metaxas is a speaker, nationally-syndicated radio host, and #1 *New York Times* bestselling author. His books have been translated into more than twenty languages, and his memorable keynote speech at the 2012 National Prayer Breakfast has been viewed over half a million times. Eric is the author of many books, including the *New York Times* bestsellers *Miracles*, *Bonhoeffer*, *Amazing Grace*, and *Seven Men*. He also was a writer for VeggieTales and has written more than thirty children's books, including the bestsellers *Squanto and the Miracle of Thanksgiving* and *It's Time to Sleep, My Love*, illustrated by Nancy Tillman. ABC News has called Eric "a photogenic, witty ambassador for faith." He lives in Manhattan with his wife and daughter. You can visit his website at www.ericmetaxas.com.